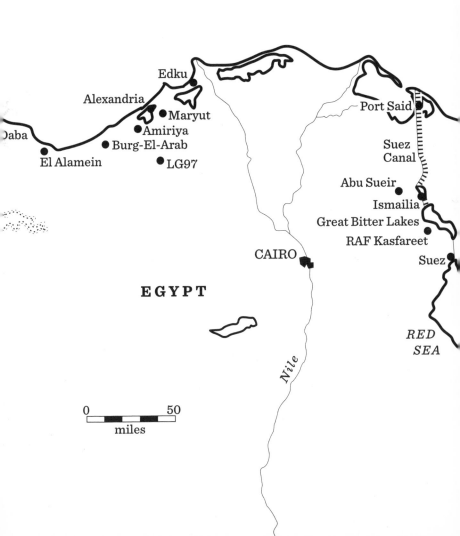

MEDITERRANEAN SEA

Edku

Alexandria

Maryut

Daba

Amiriya

Burg-El-Arab

El Alamein

LG97

Port Said

Suez Canal

Abu Sueir

Ismailia

Great Bitter Lakes

RAF Kasfareet

CAIRO

Suez

EGYPT

RED SEA

Nile

0   50
miles

PEDRO

PEDRO

The Life and Death of Fighter Ace Osgood Villiers Hanbury, DSO, DFC and Bar

ROBIN RHODERICK-JONES

GRUB STREET · LONDON

Published by
Grub Street
4 Rainham Close
London
SW11 6SS

Copyright © Grub Street 2010
Copyright text © Robin Rhoderick-Jones
Copyright foreword © Sir Christopher Lee

British Library Cataloguing in Publication Data

Rhoderick-Jones, Robin.
  Pedro : the life and death of fighter ace Osgood Villiers
  Hanbury, DFC and bar.
  1. Hanbury, Osgood Villiers. 2. Fighter pilots--Great
  Britain--Biography. 3. World War, 1939-1945--Aerial
  operations, British.
  I. Title
  940.5'44'941'092-dc22

ISBN-13: 9781906502652

Cover design by Sarah Driver
Edited by Sophie Campbell
Formatted by Sarah Driver

Printed and bound by MPG Ltd, Bodmin, Cornwall

Grub Street Publishing only uses
FSC (Forest Stewardship Council) paper for its books.

CONTENTS

Foreword

PEDRO

This is what he was called by everybody in the Desert Air Force. He was widely known for his courage and passion for combat, especially against the Germans. 260 Squadron were very proud of him and his achievements; he rightly deserved the decorations he earned.

To look at, he was the very antithesis of a fighting man. He was reasonably tall, very thin, large eyes and a moustache that could have been taken from the current famous cartoon of Two Types. It was most representative of Desert Air Force during our campaigns: we wore corduroy trousers, no rank badges, battered caps and enormous moustaches. I believe Pedro would have loved to dress like that. His moustache was certainly large. I remember when I joined the squadron, he said to me 'one mistake and you're out; now let's go and get pissed'. He was quite good at that too.

I know he went to Eton College and distinctly remember he told me once he'd been expelled for some reason, it wasn't entirely clear. I can't vouch for the truth of that, but why make it up? He wasn't that kind of person.

It was a terrible blow to the squadron and entire Desert Air Force when he and our wing commander Billy Burton were shot down on the way back from a brief holiday. Nobody knows why. Some think the Germans were after the Air Office Commander of Desert Air Force, Harry Broadhurst. But we shall never know.

I personally have very fond memories of a remarkable, amusing and immensely brave man and it is a tragedy to us all that he died in such a futile way. He always enjoyed taking risks and I truly believe in a strange way he actually loved the war.

I will never forget him. I wish this book every success and best wishes to his son, Christopher

Christopher Lee
London, December 2009

Chapter One

THE LEGACY

 602 Squadron RAF
Sunday 15 September 1940

'Dear Mummy and Dad,
Have had a very busy day having been
up on four one-hour patrols. We had a fine
battle this afternoon when twelve of us ran
*into eighteen Dorniers [*the Dornier Do17,
a German bomber with a crew of between
three and five*] for once unescorted by*
fighters. We got three certainties and sev-
eral probables. I picked one out and was
just diving to do a head-on attack when it
went down, hit by another of our fighters. I
followed it down to make sure it crashed

and, after cruising around just above the sea I saw a Dornier 17 flying parallel with me just below the clouds. I went into the cloud and went flat out for a few minutes, turned, and as I dived out my luck was in and I got him head-on. He went straight into the sea and I am glad to say there were no survivors.

'I stayed in the district for about a quarter of an hour and saw Germans who had bailed out fall into the sea – including one whose parachute had not opened. I also saw a British fighter dive in but I believe the pilot had bailed out. A Dornier which had blown up came floating down in bits and another burnt up on land. It was a most spectacular show.

'I have not much time now to tell you about the squadron. Yes they were on the Firth [of Forth] raid. Their past commanding officers include the Duke of Hamilton, the Everest flyer, and Squadron Leader MacIntyre, the commanding officer at Prestwick when I was there.

'We have so far accounted for sixty-three confirmed Huns for a loss of three pilots killed and about ten wounded which is a pretty good average. I am afraid leave is out of the question.

Must fly!
Love to all,

Tiggy.

THE LEGACY

Stationed at Westhampnett in Sussex, Pilot Officer Osgood Villiers Hanbury, aged twenty-three and fresh from his officer's training unit, had made his first kill in the Battle of Britain.

He had been known as Tiggy for as long as he could remember, his elder sister Rachel having fancied that as a baby he resembled Mrs Tiggy-Winkle the hedgehog and a favourite character from the books of the newly fashionable Beatrix Potter. This family joke was to follow him throughout his schooldays and on into his brief commercial career before his friends in the RAF re-christened him with a name more to their own inventive tastes.

Hanbury is a name of old English or Anglo-Saxon derivation meaning high fortress, and the first of Tiggy's ancestors to come to light was Roger de Hanbury, who in 1182 was living in a settlement of that name near Droitwich in Worcestershire. The fact that Roger and his brother Guy were named in the French format does not necessarily mean that they were of Norman descent, although both Christian names were commonly found in Normandy. The family was not to shed the 'de' until the fifteenth century.

From Worcestershire the Hanburys spread into Wales, members of the family settling around the Monmouthshire village of Pontypool and the neighbouring parishes of Llanfihangel, Panteg and Pontymoel. In the seventeenth century they had made such progress that Capel Hanbury (1625-1704) had become an acknowledged pioneer of the tin-plate industry and master of more than one ironworks. In 1698 Capel was followed into Wales by his kinsman, Philip, whose family had lived in Elmley Lovett, some 5 miles from the principal family house known by then as Hanbury Hall. Philip first acquired property in Llanfihangel but finally settled in Panteg. He was succeeded by his eldest son Richard, who lived in Pontymoel (now a suburb of Pontypool) and became one of the earliest and most prominent Quakers. His house became the local Friends Meeting Place and the garden became a Quaker cemetery. The family remained Quakers for at least six generations before joining the Anglican faith.

Richard's great-grandson, John Hanbury (born in 1700), left Wales and moved to London where he built up a successful business dealing in Virginia tobacco, becoming one of the most prominent tobacco merchants in Europe. At thirty he married Anne Osgood (another Quaker) whose father Henry's estate was at Holfield Grange, near Coggeshall in Essex. When Henry died the estate came into John Hanbury's possession.

John did not confine himself entirely to trade. He played an important role in developing Virginia as a thriving colony, buying 500,000 acres of land and helping to settle around 100 Quaker families. This settlement became the scene of fierce fighting between the French and the Virginians to such an extent that in 1755 British Army reinforcements had to be despatched from England, one contingent travelling in a transport ship owned by Hanbury and named the *Osgood*. A combined force of British and Colonials was assembled and, commanded by Lieutenant Colonel George Washington, the Virginian element was ignominiously defeated by the French; it was not until 1760 that Hanbury's lands were reclaimed for the settlers. By this time both John and Anne had died, leaving Holfield and the tobacco business to their only son, Osgood.

Osgood Hanbury took on his father's affairs and became a family man, marrying Mary (Molly) Lloyd of the Birmingham banking family and producing five sons and three daughters. When John, the eldest boy died, his brother Osgood became the next in line and he duly inherited Holfield in 1784. This Osgood married Susannah Barclay, daughter of John, a London banker. In the wake of the American Revolution and the consequent uncertainty over trade, Osgood left the tobacco business and became a banker, co-founding the City firm Barnett, Hoare, Hanbury and Lloyd. He and Susannah had ten children and it was their fifth son Philip, born in 1802, who, having married Elizabeth Collot d'Escury, daughter of a Dutch baron, was to be Tiggy's great-grandfather.

In addition to the tin-plate, tobacco and banking industries, pharmacy, gardening and brewing also came to play prominent roles in Hanbury history. Daniel Bell Hanbury, born in 1794 and a direct descendant of Capel, founded the Pharmaceutical Society and joined William Allen, another Quaker, the dominant partner of a pharmaceutical manufacturing company founded in the early eighteenth century. Allen's daughter married Daniel's brother Cornelius and the firm now known as Allen and Hanbury's became well-known all over the world: it was still trading globally in the twentieth century until absorbed by Glaxo in 1958.

Daniel's third son, Thomas, born in 1832, became a Shanghai silk-merchant but at heart was a botanist. In 1837 he created the celebrated garden at La Mortola in Italy and, later, the Genoa Botanical Institute. In 1902 he bought the Wisley estate in Surrey, including the Oakwood garden created by George Wilson, presenting it the following year to the Royal Horticultural Society in trust for the society's perpetual use. At the other end of the country, Philip and Elizabeth's daughter, Mary, had married (as his second wife) Sir Francis Mackenzie of Gairloch, and it was their son, Osgood Hanbury Mackenzie, who founded at Inverewe on the north-west coast of Scotland, one of the world's greatest exotic gardens.

THE LEGACY

Brewing came into the Hanbury family when Sampson, son of the first Osgood of Holfield Grange, became a partner in the Old Truman Brewery in 1789 when he was only twenty, being joined soon afterwards by his brother Osgood. Sampson was a larger-than-life character (he later weighed over 17 stones) who acquired the Poles estate in Hertfordshire and became famous in three counties as Master of the Puckeridge Foxhounds, gaining praise from Surtees himself who considered Hanbury as knowing more about hound breeding than anyone in England. Old Truman ales had been produced at premises in Brick Lane in London since 1666, but by the time Sampson and his nephew Thomas Buxton, son of Sampson's sister Anna, had improved the brewing process and converted the works to steam-power, Old Truman had become Truman, Hanbury, Buxton and Company and was among the biggest brewing companies in England. Sampson's descendents, together with those of Osgood and Thomas Buxton, took their turn at Truman until well into the twentieth century – in 1886 there were as many as three Hanburys and four Buxtons on the board.

Philip Hanbury, however, had followed his father into Barnett, Hoare, Hanbury and Lloyd, remaining a banker for fifty-six years. He and Elizabeth lived at Woodlands, Redhill, where he became a Justice of the Peace and a much respected citizen of the county of Surrey. Philip and Elizabeth died within ten months of each other, she first in September 1877 and Philip in July the following year. Their marriage had produced seven sons and a daughter. The fifth boy, born, rather surprisingly in Clapham on 28 March 1852 was baptised Ernest Osgood. In May 1875, Ernest married Clara Martha, daughter of Rose and John Whitehead, a hop factor originally of Ladds Court at Chart Sutton, near Maidstone where Clara was born, but then of Brixton in London. The newly-married Hanburys set up home in a house called The Firs at Teston, a village near Maidstone, and in the fifteen years before their divorce in 1890 had six children, the eldest boy, Philip, being born at home on 5 June 1879.

Despite his banking heritage, Ernest Hanbury had been drawn towards brewing as a career, joining The Kent Brewery in Bow Road, Wateringbury only 4 miles from Teston. The Kent Brewery had been founded by John Beal Jude in 1840 but by 1878 was trading as Jude Hanbury & Company and had adopted Invicta, the White Horse of Kent, as its trademark. Its two directors were Ernest and John Dunstan Whitehead, Clara's brother, who was conveniently to marry Ernest's niece, Elfrida Hanbury. In an era when family breweries were sprouting up all over the country, Jude Hanbury more than held its own, commissioning agents in many parts of the county as well as in Sussex and in London. They also opened offices and stores in Tunbridge Wells and by the time Jude Hanbury was converted into a limited company in 1919, it owned some 200 public houses. Ernest's business was an undoubted success - much more so than his personal life. His marriage had been less than harmonious and its breaking up was fraught: when he learnt that his wife intended to divorce him he is reputed to have driven a flock of sheep through their drawing room in protest.

In November 1896, having spent some time living with his younger brother, Albert, in Staplehay, near Taunton in Somerset, Ernest married Lucy Anne Edwards who came from Lancashire. Albert and another brother, Theodore, were also brewers, having bought the Cannon Street Brewery in Taunton. However when Albert died in June 1893, Ernest moved to Worthing where he and Lucy settled in a modest house called Amatola, employing only one servant – a distinct down-sizing from his years at The Firs where in 1881, he, Clara and the children enjoyed the services of a cook, parlourmaid, two nursery maids and a groom. How and where Philip and his four siblings – brother Selby and sisters, Cecile, Gladys and Dorothy (another girl, Muriel, had died aged seven in 1883) – were brought up after their parents' divorce is not clear, but it is likely that they spent most, if not all, of their most formative years with Clara. Certainly no children are recorded as being with Ernest during the 1891 census when he was living with Albert.

When young Philip Hanbury came of age at the turn of the century, he decided that he would not – immediately at any rate – follow his father into Jude Hanbury. Instead he travelled to Ceylon (later Sri Lanka) where he became a tea-planter on the Kanapediwatte estate at Ulapane in the

Central Highlands, some 60 miles north-east of the capital, Colombo.

In 1907, while on leave with relatives in Scarborough, he joined the part-time army, securing a commission as a second-lieutenant in a reserve battalion of Princess Alexandra of Wales's Own Yorkshire Regiment, later to become The Green Howards. He seems not to have been called up for any period of active service for the next seven years, although Selby, who later also became a tea-planter in Ceylon, served in Royston's Horse, a South African mounted regiment formed specifically to help put down the Zulu rebellion in Natal in 1906. At that time Selby was only twenty but was soon to distinguish himself as an adventurer by riding alone from Cape Town to Nairobi, reputedly cuddling up against his horse at night to ward off the cold.

No account survives of Philip's time in Ceylon, but planters seem to have led a life during which long periods of loneliness were interspersed with frantic socialising at the nearest British club and rare excursions to Kandy and Colombo. It is entirely possible that it was during one of these breaks from his plantation solitude that Philip met Dorothy Maude (Dodo) Margary, daughter of Henry Villiers Margary and his wife Catherine, who lived in Haputale, a spectacularly situated town perched on the southern ridge of the Highlands – a journey of around 60 miles from Ulapane. The Margary family had been in and around India for some time, Henry's father being Major General Henry Joshua Margary of the

Royal Engineers who had spent most of his service in the sub-continent. The old general, who had been born in 1811 and fathered sixteen children with his wife Louisa, died in 1876 at Weston-super-Mare 'of excessive grief', brought about by the death of a son, Augustus, a celebrated diplomat and sinologist who had been murdered a year earlier by Chinese at Manwein while surveying a route from Upper Burma to Shanghai.

The younger Henry was the eldest son of the general's large family and he and Catherine were married in Ceylon in 1877, eventually producing seven children of whom Dodo, born in 1886, was the youngest. She was twenty-seven years old when in November 1913 she married Philip Hanbury at St Michael's and All Angels church in Colombo. Her father had died some years previously and she was given away by her uncle, another planter, Catherine's brother Nathaniel Orchard, and attended by her sister Evelyn. Philip's best man was his brother Selby and the reception took place in a private dining room of the Galle Face Hotel. The honeymoon was spent in Kandy, but now their life as planters was coming to an end as the clouds of war gathered over Europe and Philip felt that his duty lay with his country and with his regiment.

They returned to England and by the outbreak of war, he had become a senior lieutenant and been called up for full-time service at the Yorkshire Regiment's depot in Richmond. He spent some time being trained for war and then in training reservists before, in 1915, he was promoted to captain and on 12 April was drafted with a party of 200 men to join the 2nd Battalion on the front line in France. Within a month he was in the trenches and in August he was commanding C Company.

Dodo was by now pregnant with their first child and living at 30 Newbiggin in Richmond. She and her husband had convinced themselves that they were to have a boy and this thought was some comfort to Philip as he wrote to his wife what he thought might easily be a last letter. Poignant as it was, it was also practical, addressing Dodo's financial position and making suggestions as to how she might make the most of widowhood:

17 May 1915

'*My darling Dodo,*
I am just off to the firing line and want to write a few lines in case I get knocked on the head. In the first place I love you better than anybody in the world and think you have been a perfect angel.

'*Well you must promise me that you will try and not grieve too much. There will be hundreds and hundreds of people in the same boat and you will have your little baby which I am sure will be a very nice little baby and you may call him Philip as well as Osgood Villiers or Philip Villiers Osgood would sound better.*'

THE LEGACY

There now follows a detailed account of the financial arrangements he had put in hand if he was killed, forecasting for her a total income of some £400 a year. The letter then continues:

'And, my dear, if in years to come you should meet someone whom you thought was nearly – not quite – as nice as me, you must marry him. You have made me very happy and there is no reason why you should not make someone else happy too. If possible you should have your own house – even if it is a cottage – and if anybody else lives there they are living with you and not you with them. It will give you more interest in life and you are a very capable young thing.

'Get a copy of the H[anbury] family [tree] and write it up to date and rummage about and find out all about families that belong to you as I like doing. You may also take up fishing if you get near a trout stream. Read some of Sir Ed Grey's [Sir Edward Grey, later Viscount Grey of Fallodon] works on fly-fishing – I want P.V.O.H to be a fisherman. They say that if a man is a fisherman he is never altogether bad! P.V.O.H need not go into the army because his father was not a soldier but a planter, but if he does anything else he might join some old thing, Volunteers, Yeomanry – anything in case he is wanted.

PEDRO

'You know I did not really want to come out here from the beginning but I am very thankful that I did. I pity anybody who hasn't done something he might have done. God Bless darling. We'll meet again.

Philip.'

As it turned out he not only survived the war, but lived until he was seventy-six. Their first child, however, was not P. V. O. H. as he had forecast, but a girl, Rachel Osgood, born in St Andrew's in Scotland, the home of Dodo's youngest Margary aunt, Anna, wife of Harold Wilson. Rachel's arrival came barely two months after her father's departure and it was to be another two years before the hoped-for son was born.

By the time of Tiggy's birth in Richmond on 13 September 1917, Philip had gained a Mention-in-Despatches and had been engaged in desperate battles at Fromelles, Festubert and – worst of all – Loos, where the battalion lost six officers (including two out of the four in Hanbury's company) and thirty-two soldiers. In April 1916 he was promoted to temporary major but soon afterwards fell ill and was repatriated to one of the territorial companies of the 3rd (Special Reserve) Battalion of his regiment stationed in West Hartlepool. His severe bronchitis, complicated by several bouts of influenza and at least one of pneumonia, were the subject of several medical boards which resulted in the granting to him of extended periods of sick and convalescent leave during which he and

Dodo spent some time with the Wilsons in St Andrews at an address which the military authorities accused him of concealing! As Philip was later to point out with some force, the War Office was mistaken – a letter he wrote to them in August is clearly headed by his Scottish address.

Hanbury's health hardly improved during the next eighteen months. He was variously described as underweight, breathless and easily exhausted. Nevertheless he was eventually passed fit for home service and posted to Neasham, near Darlington, as Commandant of the Musketry School during which time the family lived at Hurworth Cottage in Hurworth-on-Tees. When this job came to an end he saw out the rest of the war as adjutant of the 3rd Battalion in Richmond from where he sporadically engaged the War Office in postal battles over the question of his rank. He was able to demonstrate that his temporary majority had never been officially relinquished despite his reversion to captain for his last job – a fact which was eventually, but reluctantly, conceded by the authorities. On 3 June 1919, while imminently expecting a third child (Elizabeth Cecile, known as Betty, was to be born in July) and living at Mote Hall, Bearstead, near Maidstone, he was demobilized and joined his father in Jude Hanbury. His return to civilian life did not, however, mark the end of his military liability; his official discharge did not come until his fiftieth birthday on 5 June 1929 when he reached the age limit for service in the reserve forces, and retired in the honorary rank of major.

For someone who had joined the militia (later the Territorial Army) not as a result of a calling but merely out of a sense of duty to his country, Philip Hanbury had more than done his bit. No doubt, had his health not given out, he would have spent the last eighteen months of the war in the trenches with a considerably enhanced chance of being killed.

Chapter Two

BETWEEN THE WARS

Osgood Villiers Hanbury weighed in at birth at a healthy 7lbs and 9ozs (3½ kilograms). His hair was fair and straight, his eyes were blue and his eyelashes long. On 29 October he was christened at the Parish Church of St Mary the Virgin in Richmond, his godparents being Ethel Bignell (Dodo's sister), Major Claude Sheppard of the 53rd Sikhs and Captain W. H. Murray of the Scottish Rifles. He was an advanced baby, speaking his first word 'Dad' at six months and standing unaided just before his first birthday, by which time his favourite word was 'more'! More was also a sentiment subscribed to by his parents because Rachel, Tiggy and Betty were soon to be joined by two sisters: Cecile Priscilla (Doddy) in 1921 and Philippa Dorothea in 1924, both born at Mote Hall.

PEDRO

Tiggy, aged five in 1922, with three of his
sisters – a fourth sister, Philippa, was to be
born in 1924. Rachel, the eldest at seven, stands
behind while, from the left, sit Tiggy, Cecile
Priscilla (Doddy) and Elizabeth Cecile (Betty).

During the year following Philippa's birth the
family moved to an imposing dower house,
Updown, rented from Lord Northbourne of
Betteshanger. Updown, south of the village of
Eastry, about halfway to Betteshanger, had its
own cricket ground fashioned 100 years earlier,
and Tiggy as he grew up, took great delight in
showing it off to his friends.

The first board meeting of Jude Hanbury as an
incorporated limited company was held at 19
Eastcheap on 3 November 1919 during which

John Quiller Rowett, John Dunstan Whitehead and Major Philip Hanbury were appointed directors with Rowett as chairman. The company's solicitors were to be Hanbury, Whitting and Ingle (another family connection) and the registered office remained at Wateringbury.

John Rowett was an extraordinary man who had made a fortune in the wine and spirits industry. After the war he became a notable contributor to public and charitable causes, especially hospitals. He co-founded the Rowett Research Institute in Aberdeen and wholly financed the polar explorer Ernest Shackleton's final expedition to Antarctica. Shackleton lost his life on that voyage and Rowett acquired his whale-boat, the *James Caird*, presenting it to his and Shackleton's old school, Dulwich College.

Rowett, Whitehead and Philip Hanbury were directors for the next three years and, with Arthur Whitting, the solicitor, also acting as company secretary, it is these four men who set about building up the business. All had been allotted a substantial number of both preferential and ordinary shares. Other shareholders included Ernest who now, however, played no active part in the running of the company, Theodore Hanbury and, rather bizarrely, John Lucas Edwards of Brighton, described as a pianoforte maker! Philip Hanbury was appointed managing director and his principal roles were to see to the efficient running of the brewery and its public houses, and the inspection of potentially profitable houses owned by other businesses with a view to reporting to the board on the practicalities of acquisition. The other directors also charged Philip with conducting negotiations with rival breweries with a view either to taking them over or examining the merits of partnerships.

In 1921, Hanbury began a series of lengthy talks with Messrs F. Leney and Sons Limited, another Wateringbury company, which had expressed a keen interest in taking over Jude Hanbury. At first Philip appears to have been enthusiastic, recommending an amalgamation of the two companies with himself and a Leney director as co-managing directors, but by the summer of 1922, no acceptable agreement had been reached and the idea was dropped.

At the beginning of the following year, Hanbury was negotiating with Messrs Isherwood, Foster and Stacey Limited, a Maidstone brewery which was also expressing an interest in buying Jude Hanbury. This move, too, seems to have had Philip's support at first as he asked his fellow directors for permission to take up a further 10,000 shares in order to strengthen his position in the event of a sale. Rowett and Whitehead agreed, but shortly afterwards, in March 1923, talks with Isherwood, Foster and Stacey had come to an end as the Jude Hanbury board turned down an offer of £207,000 for all their tied houses.

Negotiations with other, similar, companies happened regularly throughout 1923, Rowett and Whitehead leaving the bargaining entirely in Philip's hands. In one such deal he instructed the solicitors to make an offer of £145,000 for the purchase of Ash's East Kent Brewery, including all their licensed and unlicensed premises together with stock, goodwill and plant. This offer had to be increased by £20,000 before the transaction could be concluded but Jude Hanbury was then able to expand in the way Philip had envisaged. There also appears to have been an almost constant stream of opportunities both to buy and sell individual licensed premises, and the family's widespread tentacles in the industry were again apparent when Truman, Hanbury, Buxton and Company made an offer for all Jude Hanbury's houses in the Chatham area. The offer amounted to £115,000 which Philip was able to increase to £125,000 before recommending acceptance to his co-directors.

In the autumn of 1923 Hanbury recommended to Rowett and Whitehead that the company's brewing operations at Wateringbury should be transferred, together with the company's offices, to the Dane John Brewery premises in Canterbury. Thus giving a much needed opportunity to modernise their equipment and enlarge its capacity to the extent that it could supply not only their current hotels and public houses but also any further acquisitions. This proposal was adopted and so delighted was Rowett by this and other successful operations, including the takeover of Tenterden Brewery Company Limited, that he proposed that Philip's salary should be increased to £2,500 (from £1,500) a year free of tax in addition to the substantial annual dividends paid on his shareholding and an annual 5% performance bonus on company net profits over £9,000.

As the year turned, an unexpected tragedy befell the board. John Whitehead died on New Year's Eve, leaving only Rowett and Hanbury to run the company until the appointment of another director in the shape of Philip's brother-in-law, Eden Gawne, chairman of the distillers John Reid Wright and Company Limited.

Worse was to follow when, in October 1924, Rowett hanged himself at his London home. Earlier that year Sir John Stewart, a Scottish whisky distiller and sole partner of Alexander Stewart & Son had shot himself because his business was heading into bankruptcy and a company in Edinburgh in which he held a large interest had already collapsed. One of Stewart's major creditors was Rowett to whom he owed £100,000. Seeing this as a sign that he himself was about to be the victim of a general downturn in his business affairs, Rowett took his own life. Shortly thereafter Philip was appointed chairman.

Despite the general malaise of the British economy following the war and the unfortunate demise of half its directors, Jude Hanbury was clearly flourishing. It was very much a family company: among the shareholders were Philip's brother Selby and their first cousin Alfred Collot Barclay Hanbury together with his sisters Cecile Gawne, Dorothy Taylor and Gladys Hanbury. Dodo's sisters and their husbands were also involved: Kitty (wife of Sir Austen Hadow, formerly such a distinguished Commissioner of Indian Railways that family lore had it that he had on occasion stood in for the viceroy), Ethel, who had married Peter Pate, and Evelyn, wife of Claude Sheppard all held shares. The chairman, too, was doing well and, although at pains never in any sense to appear flashy, Philip had acquired the trappings of a rich man, owning one, if not two, Rolls-Royce motor cars and a Daimler.

The Hanbury children enjoyed an idyllic child-hood, roaming the extensive parkland around Updown and playing on the sand dunes of Sandwich Bay only a few miles away. In September 1926, four months after the bitter General Strike in which miners from the Kent coalfields centred around Betteshanger were heavily involved, but which did not affect the Kent breweries, Tiggy was sent off to preparatory school at Wellesley House at nearby Broadstairs; he was just nine years old.

His first term's report cannot have pleased his parents: with the words 'weak' and 'untidy' occurring regularly! The headmaster however, no doubt with a sensible eye on retaining a pupil with clearly well-heeled parents, summed-up young Hanbury's performance as 'very good'. By the end of his first year Tiggy had bucked up con-siderably, so that while it was clear that he would never star academically, he was credited with try-ing hard and improving.

Among his near contemporaries were Bernard Waley-Cohen, later a distinguished Lord Mayor of London, and George Mann who went on to

Tiggy aged ten. At this time (1927) he was
at a boys' preparatory school, Wellesley House,
near Broadstairs in Kent. He was a keen
cricketer and enthusiastic member of the
school's boy scout troop. From Wellesley House
he passed the common entrance exam into
Eton to which he went in September 1930.

captain England at cricket. Tiggy, too, was a very enthusiastic cricketer (his father was later to present the school with a cup to be awarded for 'Keenness at Cricket') and eventually gained his second eleven colours while appearing occasionally for the first team, being particularly commended for his batting. He was also an enthusiastic member of the school's scout troop being picked out by the scoutmaster for special congratulations for his helpful attitude. In his final term he finished near the bottom of Form II but nevertheless managed to pass his common entrance into Eton.

During Tiggy's last year at Wellesley, momentous changes were taking place at Jude Hanbury. In April 1929 at a board meeting which was also attended by Colonel William Whitbread of the eponymous London brewers, and Kenneth Moore of Edward Moore and Sons, the Whitbread auditors, the principal matter under discussion was a proposal that Jude Hanbury should bid to acquire the whole of the preference and ordinary shares in Mackeson and Company Limited who brewed in Hythe. Whitbreads were already tied in closely with Mackesons and had taken over the production of the famous Mackesons Milk Stout, a densely sweet beer which was selling so well that it had acquired a national market too big for Mackesons to fulfil. Whitbreads, a major company with head offices in London, was therefore very much involved in the negotiations which Philip was directed to undertake.

In a matter of only a few days he was successful and Mackesons had accepted his offer. This was not quite a takeover, but more of an amalgamation which saw Whitbreads, Mackesons and Jude Hanbury operating jointly together with a number of other south-eastern breweries, including Frederick Leney and Sons. From the date of this merger Jude Hanbury board meetings were held at the Whitbread offices in Chiswell Street and Colonel Whitbread and Cecil Lubbock (also of Whitbreads) joined Hanbury's board while Philip remained both chairman and co-managing director with Sydney Neville of Whitbreads. This happy and successful state of affairs continued until 1930 when Whitbreads finally took over Jude Hanbury lock, stock and barrel. Philip maintained a senior position on the board until his contract ran out in August 1932 at which time both he and Eden Gawne resigned. All the properties still owned by Jude Hanbury were then sold, most to Mackesons for £197,000 and the remainder to Leney and Sons for £84,000.

In September 1930, at a time when his fifty-year-old father was arguably at the peak of his professional life, Tiggy joined Mr E.V. Slater's house, The Timbralls, at Eton. At just five-foot tall and slightly built, he was not physically equipped to excel at sports and neither was he gifted academically. At Slater's he messed with a boy called J. P. Lucas (whose enviable claim to fame was that by the end of his time at the school he knew by heart all the verses of both Eskimo Nell and The Good Ship Venus) and Ludovic Kennedy, later famous as a campaigning journalist and broadcaster.

Despite Lucas's assertion many years afterwards that Slater ran 'a sadistic regime', Tiggy appeared to be reasonably happy. He was an assiduous letter writer, both to his parents and to Rachel and his younger sisters as they started school. Although few of these letters now survive, of those that do, none give the impression that he was in the least bit miserable. Indeed his thoughts were usually primarily concerned with others – Rachel's transient unhappiness that she had to share a room with only one other girl at her own school caused him to write immediately in sympathy.

All the Hanbury children wrote entertaining letters to their parents and it is obvious from their tone and content that they were on very good and easy terms with Philip and Dodo – the overwhelming impression being of a happy and united family. Tiggy was especially determined that his parents should not worry about him, making light of the fact that in his second half (Etonian for term) he could find no one to mess with, hastening to tell his mother: 'I don't mind much.' This disappointment was, however, mitigated by the fact that five boys he knew and liked had come to Eton to join him, three, including George Mann, from his prep school and two he knew from home in Kent.

Tiggy entered Eton in the lower fourth, moving up to the middle fourth by the following year. In the summer of 1932 he became a member of the house cricket team, topping the bowling averages, and was again a regular in the house eleven in 1933, the last year in which he played for Slater's. During the summer holidays Slater and three teaching colleagues from the school were killed in a mountaineering accident, and in September Tiggy had to move to Mr L.S. Fortescue's who had The Corner House. Tiggy had clearly put up with Slater without facing any major problems and the same can be said of his relationship with Fortescue who also had something of a reputation as a martinet. Tiggy however, found him 'not at all strict'. This interlude was brief as in September 1934 The Corner House was taken on by the gentler Mr Brian Whitfield and it was he who saw Hanbury through his last three terms.

Earlier that year Tiggy had leave out from school to attend the wedding of his cousin, Marguerite Hadow to Lieutenant William Argles, Royal Navy, at Holy Trinity Brompton on 9 May. Marguerite's mother, Kitty, was now a widow, Sir Austen having died shortly after retiring to Hampshire four years earlier. There was a great family turnout on that day, Rachel and Philippa being bridesmaids while Major and Mrs Philip Hanbury and Mr O. V. Hanbury were listed amongst the guests. Shortly afterwards Tiggy wrote to Rachel asking her to put a shilling each way on Achtenan in the Derby – a losing bet in the event; the race being won by Windsor Lad. He also recounted to her a curious expedition with his classical tutor:

'Dr Prescott took me and Walford, the boy I mess with, to the far end of Windsor Great Park in the evening as neither of us was allowed to play cricket. We went in an old Invicta and we suddenly found that we only had ten minutes to lock-up. We touched 77 and a half miles an hour on the way back. It was quite terrifying.

'I hope we have a decent day for the 4th [4 June is a highlight of the Eton year when parents are encouraged to attend the celebrations and picnic on the playing fields]. *I have now turned wet bob* [an oarsman as opposed to dry bob which is a cricketer] *much to my disgust! Are you going to the Eton Ball or the Hurlingham Ball? If it is the Eton one I can get you tickets.*

With love from

Tiggy.'

In the winter Tiggy wrote to his sister Betty who had just begun boarding school at Southover Manor in Lewes asking her how she was getting on: 'I expect it is jolly good fun there and anyway your schooldays will pass jolly quickly. I've been here four years and it only seems like a matter of months.' He went on: 'I've been doing quite a lot of football and beagling this half, but I have unfortunately got to work very hard for the

School Certificate which is rather a sweat.' His labours paid off: at the Oxford and Cambridge Schools Examination Board in December 1934 he passed with credits in English, History, Latin, French and Elementary Mathematics.

Tiggy left Eton in July 1935, two months short of his eighteenth birthday. His progress through the school had been a trifle slow and he was never to make the Sixth Form, although there does seem to have been a plan to send him to a crammer to fit him for entrance to Cambridge. Family legend has it that his last days were spent not at The Corner House but at Updown having been sent home for being seen with a girl in a London night club. Eton, however, has no record of this event and his leaver's photograph was taken in the same way as those of his contemporaries.

Philip was now faced with the problem of what to do with his son in order to prepare him for university. Attendance at a crammer – at least at this stage – seems to have taken a back seat, but Tiggy had shown a certain aptitude for languages and so it was decided that he should spend some time in both France and Germany where he might improve his French and learn some German.

As far as Germany was concerned, there was a great deal of interest in Britain at the rise to power of the Nazi party under Adolf Hitler who, by all accounts, was making good progress in reducing unemployment and building up the country's industry and infrastructure. Young Hanbury's first stop, however, was at Tours on the Loire, long acknowledged to be the district in which the most perfect French was spoken. His living arrangements were a little primitive. He reported to Rachel that although the family he was with were friendly, there were no baths in the house so that he was forced to bathe in the Cher, a tributary of the Loire. He also seems to have spent many hours in the cinema. In a letter to his sisters, he recounted that:

> *'I have done nothing interesting at all except see fourteen films and an opera. This afternoon I saw the Bengal Lancers for the second time. We get more American and English films here, but of course they are all turned into French.*
>
> *'I am afraid that the French think they are going to have a revolution fairly short-ly which will be rather a nuisance! Also I am the only person here who backs the Abyssinians against the Italians* [Mussolini's forces had invaded Abyssinia on 3 October 1935] *which is the cause of heated arguments every day.'*

He was home for Christmas, during which he and Rachel organised a ball for the Ashley Beagles with whom they all hunted – Tiggy often whipping-in. Although his sisters rode enthusiastically, he preferred following hounds on his feet, often advising the girls that it was the best way of becoming slim! He did however have a couple of mounted days before he set off once more for

France, cub-hunting with the West Street Foxhounds on Nigger, the family pony. His real favourites among the animals at Updown though, were the springer spaniels, Ben and Jane, and Buster, a black labrador. Tiggy enjoyed shooting and there was plenty to be had around Eastry with any number of generous hosts including Lord Northbourne. He had his first day with a .410 gun aged about nine, and then graduated in his teens to a grown-up 12-bore. As an above average shot, he was not short of invitations and was regularly out with his father and a military neighbour and family friend, Lieutenant Colonel Charles Harman.

The Harmans were an Irish family of the protestant ascendancy, and Charles Cecil Harman, son of William and Emily (formerly O'Rourke) of Crossdrum, near Oldcastle in County Meath, was born on 23 August 1877 and educated at Coleraine and Trinity College, Dublin. He was a fine athlete, winning the Irish inter-universities 100 and 440 yards championships in 1899 and 1900 as well as becoming the All-Ireland military champion at 440 yards in 1899, and again in 1905 and 1906.

Having been in the Officers Training Corps at Trinity he was able to enlist in 1900 as a second-lieutenant in the Leinster Regiment and was shipped off almost immediately to South Africa to join the 1st Battalion which was engaged in the Second Boer War. In common with all the officers who had come straight from university, he was known by those who had joined by the more orthodox route through the Royal Military College Sandhurst, as a 'fraud'.

From 1907 he spent four years in India with the 2nd Battalion, spending a great deal of his time shooting snipe (at which he was the regimental expert) and dancing at the officers Saturday Club – so called in the Irish way, because it met on a Friday evening! In 1911 he returned to Ireland, becoming adjutant of the 3rd Battalion in Cork before rejoining the 2nd Battalion soon after it deployed to France in September 1914. But before his departure for the front there was the matter of his wedding. On 21 October he married Muriel Huth, daughter of Percival Huth of Freshford Manor, Bath.

By May 1915, the now Lieutenant-Colonel Harman was in command of the Leinsters, hardly ever leaving the front and gaining a DSO in 1916 and another in 1918. He also had four Mentions-in-Despatches and was awarded a brevet lieu-tenant-colonelcy – all for the most gallant actions. Not all his decorations came when he was with his regiment: by the end of the war he had also commanded the 13th Battalion of the Royal Sussex Regiment and the 4th Battalion of the Bedfordshire Regiment, with whom he won the Bar to his DSO. There could hardly have been a senior officer who saw more action at first hand.

On 31 July 1922, in the wake of the partition of Ireland, the Leinster Regiment, in common with all those famous regiments raised in the twenty-six counties of Southern Ireland over the previous two and a half centuries, was disbanded. In

The officers of the 1st Battalion of the Royal
Sussex Regiment in Dover circa 1930. The battalion
was commanded by Lieutenant Colonel Charles
Harman DSO and Bar, who had transferred in on
the disbandment of the Leinster Regiment in 1922.
Lieutenant Colonel Harman sits fourth from the left
in the front row. In 1943, and living back in
Ireland, he became Pedro's father-in-law.

November of the same year Charlie Harman, as
he was known to his friends, transferred to the
Royal Sussex in the rank of major, a move which
brought him to south-east England, first at the
Senior Officers School in Woking and then to the
1st Battalion of the Royal Sussex which, as a lieutenant colonel, he commanded from 1928 until his
retirement from the army in 1932. The battalion
was stationed at Grand Shaft Barracks, Dover as a
unit of 12 Infantry Brigade commanded by

Brigadier Sir Hereward Wake. Wake had two sons who were both at Eton: one, also called Hereward, a year older than Tiggy, and Roger who was a year younger. The brigadier, Charlie Harman and Philip Hanbury often shot together and the three families became friends to such an extent that after leaving school, Tiggy spent the occasional weekend with the Wakes when they moved to Northamptonshire.

During the colonel's post-war service with the Royal Sussex, the Harman family lived at Scawsby House which also belonged to the Northbourne estate and was tucked away in a wood between Updown House and Betteshanger. The Harmans had three children, a daughter, Cecil Patricia born in 1915, quaintly so called because Charlie had badly wanted a son and thought not unnaturally that he might well be killed before one appeared. In the event, the Harmans later produced two boys: William in 1916 and Nigel in 1921.

Although Patricia (she never used her first given name) was two years older than Tiggy, they became great friends, so much so that in their teenage years an understanding grew up between them. Neither the Hanbury nor the Harman parents approved of this blossoming romance, however innocent, believing that both were too young – in particular Tiggy. Young Hanbury was, however, smitten to such a degree that on one occasion he was reported as having threatened Charlie Harman with a shot-gun when the colonel refused to allow Patricia out of the house to meet him. Sometime later the Harmans left Kent and returned to Crossdrum, the family home in Ireland. The two incidents were not, however, related!

In April 1936, after a few months at Updown, Tiggy travelled by train to Munich, the principal city of Bavaria and the ideological core of the Nazi party where Adolf Hitler had begun his surge for political power three years earlier. Tiggy's home for the next few months was to be in 16 Konradstrasse, the home of Graf [Duke] von Podewil, an aristocratic scholar, his wife the Gräfin, and their married son, Clemens. The von Podewils had fallen on hard times, supplementing their income by taking in paying guests, mainly from England and teaching them to speak German. When Tiggy arrived there were already four English girls in the students' apartment but far from being pleased, he was, he wrote, relieved to escape their 'incessant chatter' by being temporarily billeted in the flat beneath. He was also surprised to find an Eton master there 'polishing up his German'.

Money was also tight in the Hanbury household. Sometime after his departure from brewing Philip had been persuaded to invest in an American film company and had unwisely put, not only his own eggs into that one basket, but those of his wife and two of his friends. The venture failed spectacularly and the Hanburys found themselves bereft of capital and barely able to survive on Philip's income. The Rolls and the Daimler had to go, Philippa was taken away from her school (Doddy being just able to finish her

Tiggy at seventeen, on a summer climbing
expedition on the Zugspitze mountain in
southern Germany. He returned home for
Christmas 1936.

education at Southover) and Tiggy, for whom the prospect of a university education had now evaporated, became for the first time in his life, conscious of an urgent need to economise. That he took his family's unwelcome financial circumstances extremely seriously is constantly reflected in his letters home.

Neither Munich nor Germany itself were entirely to his taste although he clearly did his best to enjoy himself, swimming in both the city's baths and on expeditions to the Tegernsee, a lake some 50 kilometres south of Munich, and climbing at Garmisch-Partenkirchen and on the Zugspitze, the country's highest mountain. He had also taken a shine to Munich's beer and its largest drinking hall, the Hofbräuhaus, scene of Hitler's first proclamation of Nazi policies sixteen years earlier. He reported to his mother that: '....it holds a thousand people and it is very amusing talking to whoever you sit next to. One finds every sort of German there, Prussians, Bavarians, Austrians and many others. The amount of beer they put down is amazing. They all have bellies like barrels.'

Tiggy preferred the company of Clemens and another German friend, the son of a schoolmaster, to that of the steady stream of English students in the city. Even when four young men who had been with him in Slater's at Eton and whom he clearly liked, called, he was relieved when they left. He was so incensed when two male friends of Rachel asked him to 'fix them up with some dames' that, having directed them to the nearest nightclub, he wrote to his sister and asked her not to tell people where to find him!

Tiggy's preoccupation with his family's finances led him to seek ways in which his mother might make some money by taking in German students who wanted to spend time in England. This was not easy: the German government was not keen for its citizens to travel abroad and so export reichmarks, but with the help of the Gräfin, he found both an office that would arrange an advantageous exchange rate and a girl who would like to go to Updown:

'.....she is over twenty and speaks a fair amount of English and would not, I think require lessons. She likes tennis, bathing and riding and is fairly well off. The way to arrange it would be for her parents to pay for some of my fees here while she was with you. It would be a great saving. [A few weeks later he had found two more girls who would like to stay for a while in Kent]... *Both like the country and animals and would not want much entertaining, though I expect they would like to go about with Rachel a bit if she did not mind. But you must let me know as soon as possible so that I can arrange it all. It means a saving of a good £100.'*

Tiggy's efforts to save expense also led him to spend the last six weeks in Germany at Kreuth; a mountain village near the Tegernsee. Here he found an agreeable family who put him up at a cheaper rate than that charged by the von Podewils and with whom he got on famously. He spent his time talking to the locals, swimming and climbing in the mountainous border between Germany and Austria. The summer was hot, the people friendly and he was idyllically happy. His Kreuth hostess, too, was pleased with her guest. So impressed was she by Tiggy's manners and friendliness that she wrote to Dodo in English to sing his praises:

> 'We are quite sorry that Tiggy has left us. He is such a nice companion and not a bit giving us the impression of living with a stranger. Tiggy has always been thoughtful of all our habits of living and has even been helping to do some work in our little garden! From the beginning we liked him and hope he liked to be with us. He has been very busy here about his German and so we hope he will have nicely improved.'

In his own letters home he occasionally touched on politics. He was obviously irked that all letters leaving Germany for destinations abroad were opened at the frontier and had been warned by the von Podewils that it would go ill with them if he should criticise any aspect of the Nazi regime. In deference to their wishes (and safety) he contented himself with a single reference to the constant camouflaged military traffic patrolling the city and a rather incautious, if prescient, observation that 'one can't help feeling that they [the Germans] would not really object to another world war. They have a sort of fighting kink in their nature which seems difficult for them to dispose of.' He also reported that he had met someone who had been in a concentration camp: 'and they don't sound particularly pleasant'. He was not to know that Dachau with its gas-chambers already in operation was just up the road. Despite his reservations about the developments in Germany, however, there was at this time no real hint of the hatred of "the Hun" which was to consume him later.

As his time in Germany drew to a close, he became a little anxious about what he was to do when he returned home. 'Has Daddy', he wrote to his mother in September, 'said anything as to what is to become of me? If I am not going to Cambridge, ought we not to do something about Shell or Imperial Chemicals or whatever it is?' In the event he began work early in 1937 as a clerk in the aviation section of the Asiatic Petroleum Company, a subsidiary of Royal Dutch Shell, at its offices in St Helen's Court in the City. In his department he was astonished to find a slightly older man with two tin legs whose name, he soon discovered, was Douglas Bader. Bader had been in the RAF and in 1931 had crashed an aircraft while doing aerobatics rather too close to the ground. Although they had little in common – Bader's sporting passion was golf, a game which did not at all appeal to Tiggy – they became friends and Douglas, on at least one occasion came to stay at Updown. That experience nearly cost the Hanburys the services of their house-maid as she fled in terror on chancing upon Bader's legs hanging from the back of a chair. But the combination of working in an aviation environment and Douglas's boundless enthusiasm for flying and the RAF rubbed off on the young Hanbury.

Whilst at Shell, Tiggy lived in a bed-sitting room at 76 Cromwell Road where he was looked after by his landlady. Financial ends proved difficult to meet and he was grateful for any windfall. In a letter home in which he bemoaned the news of the loss of his beloved labrador Buster and the fact that 'it is beastly dull up here', he also told his mother that he had been persuaded to go to a greyhound track 'and I won four guineas on my system. I shall not go again for a long time but the spoils went to my landlady – much to her surprise.' Things were obviously also tight at home. In the same letter he added 'Could you send me my bathing things? I am thinking of bathing in the Serpentine. I will send you the postage.'

Tiggy's dislike of his job, his lodgings and London in general, made it very important that he should escape to the country as often as possible. He played a little tennis at the Shell Lensbury Club at Teddington but his favourite activity was wildfowling, in which his closest and most constant companion was Charles Coles, a man of his own age who worked in the ICI offices on Millbank and whom he met in 1936. Coles had an uncle who lived in Suffolk in whom he confided one day that he had never shot a goose. His uncle, a retired colonel, rose to the bait and took his nephew to Stiffkey on the Norfolk coast. This first hunting trip proved such a success that they soon went again. They tried their luck with the morning flight, before breakfast at the village pub, then set off for the marshes to walk up mallard, curlew – or indeed anything that was both shootable and edible. As they arrived they noted two men, immediately written off by the peppery colonel as 'scruffy looking chaps', emerging from the undergrowth. The colonel, not liking the look of them, carefully locked his car, observing as he did so that 'you can't tell who anybody is these days'. Back at the pub for a pre-dinner drink in the tap room, the same two disreputable figures entered. Rather doubtfully the colonel asked them how they had got on and would they like a drink. So began a long friendship, for one of the men was Tiggy and he and Charles hit it off immediately.

Coles and Hanbury quickly formed a tightly-knit group which called itself "The Creek Crawlers Club", establishing its headquarters at the Bentinck's Arms in West Lynn. Membership was sometimes a matter of some dispute. Mostly the group was drawn from the ranks of young professional men from London starting out on careers in business or the law but the man who became the key organiser of their wild-fowling activities was an outsider, Dennis Guiseppi, an accountant who lived in Cambridge and who had been dismissed by Tiggy on first acquaintance as 'that bloody wop'. Dennis was, however, by far the best shot amongst them, never returning with an empty bag and Tiggy, together with all his fellow members soon embraced this little Englishman of Italian extraction as one of their own. It helped, perhaps, that almost alone of all the "Creek Crawlers", he appeared to have plenty of money!

The club's proceedings soon became something of a ritual. Initially there were only two rules: 'A member shall be a true wildfowler' and: 'No teetotaller shall be admitted'. But they also formulated a system of fines which ensured that the bar at the Bentinck Arms – where they were trusted to keep their own tally by chalking up the rounds on a blackboard – was kept busy. Failure to get up in time for the morning flight cost five pints of beer while for running out of cartridges or taking another member's bird the penalty was only one. Wounding another member cost two rounds of port while killing one (never put to the test!) rated two rounds of brandy and payment of the undertakers' fee. Twice a year they dined at Stone's Chop House in Panton Street, just off the Haymarket in London, where outstanding fines were collected and paid in liquid form.

The "Creek Crawlers" day was long and almost always arduous. After the morning flight and breakfast, sandwiches were taken back out on the marshes. Sea mists came up quickly and flood tides were frequent, burying the few landmarks, so that compass and torch were vital pieces of equipment. If anyone fell into the freezing waters it was a matter of honour to keep going all day and into the evening flight before any move could be made towards a bath and change of clothing. It was a tough school which stood the members in good stead when the war came and bodily discomfort was a way of life. Charles Coles was a naval reservist but oddly he and Tiggy's paths were to cross again – but some thousands of miles from the Bentinck Arms.

In 1938 came the first Hanbury family wedding when Rachel married Captain Henry Harland in St John's Cathedral in Hong Kong where he was serving with the Royal Scots. They had announced their engagement in May, shortly before Hector (the name by which Harland was always known) sailed for the Far East, and were married in October. The possible outbreak of war – and presumably the shortage of funds – precluded the presence of Philip and Dodo or any of Rachel's siblings so that she was given away by Harland's commanding officer, Lieutenant Colonel Hall. Missing his eldest sister's wedding was a matter of huge regret for Tiggy. But by this time he was preparing for war.

Chapter Three

LEARNING TO FLY

The Auxiliary Air Force (AAF) came into being in 1924 to supplement the still young RAF in the same way as the Territorial Army complemented the regular regiments and corps of the British Army. As initially conceived the AAF was expected, within two years, to raise twenty-five squadrons, numbering from 600 Squadron upwards, and were to be the responsibility of county organisations known as the Territorial Army and Air Force Associations. Compared with other non-regular components of the RAF (such as the Special Reserve), the AAF had a number of advantages: it employed relatively few (expensive) regulars and, because of a high degree of local support, the squadrons were well recruited and morale was high. It would also be true to say that, rather like the fashionable county Yeomanry cavalry regiments, the recruiting of pilots was largely confined to those of a social status which ensured that they would be considered suitable for immediate commissioning to officer rank – in other words they would 'fit-in'. This led to a public school exclusivity which caused one applicant who later became a famous World War Two fighter ace, to be turned down because he did not hunt! It also meant that for most of the period leading up to the war the AAF had no NCO (non commissioned officer) pilots.

The auxiliaries would have been a natural home for someone of Tiggy's background but by the mid-1930s its deficiencies had been giving the RAF some cause for concern. In particular the Director of RAF Training, the then Air Commodore Arthur Tedder, was critical of the restrictive nature of the bonds which tied the AAF to county associations and its lack of NCO pilots. It was these misgivings which led Tedder to initiate the formation of the Royal Air Force Volunteer Reserve (RAFVR) in 1936. The RAFVR had a wider social base than the AAF and its budding pilot volunteers were required to commit to serving full time in the event of a national emergency. Entry was to be at the lowest rank (aircraftsman class 2) with promotion to sergeant the following day. Commissions were to be available to all who subsequently proved their worth. The RAFVR soon came to contain men from a wide range of educational backgrounds and Tedder's concept developed so successfully that by the outbreak of war in September 1939, there were some 5,000 RAFVR pilots on the books. Relatively few, however, had yet been trained to the level demanded by air combat.

In June 1938 Tiggy had made up his mind to join the Volunteer Reserve. He had discovered that if he did so (as opposed to the AAF) a new government-sponsored scheme allowed him leave of absence from Shell on half-pay. Careful as ever over his finances, he explained to his father that he would be paid 16 shillings a day (5 pounds and 12 shillings a week) by the RAF which, when added to half his Shell salary, would bring the total up to over £7 a week – a great deal more than he was used to. 'This', he wrote, 'will be a very good opportunity for getting straight financially and, also, I am very interested in flying. I hope you have no objections.' Far from opposing his son's plan, Philip was extremely pleased.

Being accepted for flying training had taken a little longer than Tiggy anticipated, but on 19 January 1939, No. 742867 AC2 O. V. Hanbury had joined the ranks and on the 20th he had become Sergeant Hanbury (pilot under training). His enlistment medical was satisfactory, recording him as being 5 foot 11 inches in height, with a 37-inch chest, blue eyes, brown hair and a fresh complexion. His home address was given as the Lensbury Club, Broom Road, Teddington, Middlesex which was now also the offices of the Asiatic Petroleum Company which had been moved out of London. He had, however, been posted a long way from home and now found himself at No.12 Elementary and Reserve Flying Training School (ERFTS) at Prestwick aerodrome near Ayr, the home of the civilian company, Scottish Aviation. To begin with he lived on the station in a sergeant's dormitory, but as the ranks of trainees, both pilots and potential navigators swelled, he was moved out first to an attic in the town as a lodger in a private house, and then to slightly more spacious private accommodation, also in Ayr. On the morning of his first day's training he was airborne in a dual-control Tiger Moth in the company of Pilot Officer Underhill, his instructor for the next two months. No time had been wasted.

It is quite clear from his letters home that Tiggy enjoyed his life at Prestwick. After just two days, he was enthusing about his experiences:

'Car driving seems silly now compared with flying. The Tigers we are in are easy to handle and I have taken off myself seven times and done five landings. I don't feel a bit dizzy looking down from an aeroplane; it's nothing like as bad as looking down when you're climbing. Yesterday we were doing stalling which is pointing your nose at too high an angle and you slip back on your tail so you have to put your nose down and dive about 1000 feet which rather upsets your stomach but I believe you get used to it! I expect to do my first solo in about a week.'

His course had only three members of the Volunteer Reserve, the rest being short service commission pilot candidates and observers, but various other auxiliary and reservists came in to train at weekends. The work was intensive on the ground as well as in the air: there were lectures on machine gunnery, parachuting ('no jumping except in an emergency'), navigation, morse-code, signalling, weather, engines and other related subjects. But there was still time for some sport, particularly shooting on the foreshore of the Ayrshire coast: geese, mallard, teal and 'swarms of golden plover' kept him happy and provided welcome physical exercise.

On the morning of 30 January, after just over seven hours of dual instruction, he flew solo for the first time, staying airborne for fifteen minutes, and then was sent up by himself again in the afternoon to practise take-offs and landings. By 24 March he had completed sixty hours and was graded 'above average' by the chief flying instructor. He had now decided that he would like to go for a short service commission in the RAF proper. He was far from alone in making this application – the RAF had become inundated with such requests. He was sent on a month's leave, spent largely at the Lensbury Club (with frequent expeditions to the Suffolk coast) and it gradually became apparent as war appeared inevitable that it would take some time before he could become an officer. Instead he resumed flying training, this time with No. 13 Elementary and Reserve Flying Training School at White

Waltham near Maidenhead. Here he again began on the Tiger Moth before graduating in August to both the Hart Trainer and the Audax. These two types were very similar, being bi-planes made by Hawker. The Hart had been originally designed as a light bomber and the Audax as an army co-operation aircraft – although by the time Tiggy arrived at White Waltham it had largely been superseded in this role and was employed mainly as an advanced trainer.

During the four months he spent at White Waltham, Tiggy took his total number of flying hours to nearly ninety, until on 1 September, he was mobilised and entered into a period of uncertainty. Various possibilities opened up: he thought he might be posted to another training unit in the United Kingdom or, more likely, to Canada where a number of RAF pilots were now under training. He was ordered by the Air Ministry not to go further than 100 miles from London and to leave contact telephone numbers regularly. Once, with a friend, he went to see Updown House, now in the hands of new tenants. He called on them and was not impressed; he did, though, rather grudgingly acknowledge that their old pony was in good shape grazing the paddocks.

During his flying training at Prestwick and White Waltham, there had been no time to learn the basics of military life so beloved by the authorities. To make good this gap in his service career he was sent to an RAF Initial Training Wing (ITW) based at Emmanuel College, Cambridge. No. 1 ITW provided a tough environment, entirely devoid of any of the finer things of life. Drill, physical training, map-reading, route marches and weapons training figured prominently on the curriculum; warrant officers and other senior figures chivvied and chased the trainees from early morning to late at night. The fact that he was now – at least nominally – Sergeant Pilot O. V. Hanbury RAF mattered little; he might just as well have been a civilian recruit straight off the street. Accommodation was in billets equipped with wooden beds, paliasses (mattresses stuffed with straw) and tin lockers. Tiggy far from enjoyed this experience and his misery was compounded by vaccinations and inoculations which gave him a fever and a bout of 'flu during which he had to be carted off to sick-quarters on a stretcher with a temperature of 104. 'Rotten sick-quarters these', he reported to his mother, 'typical RAF; draughty, noisy, lukewarm food on cold plates'. There was little scope for sporting or social activities – although a senior officer did recruit him to escort one of his nieces to a dance!

By Christmas (spent in London, looking up friends, much to his parents' disappointment) he had finished with Cambridge and was looking forward to his next posting – this time to No. 11 Flying Training School at RAF Shawbury, near Shrewsbury, which, as he pointed out to Philip and Dodo, was really quite close to Altrincham in Cheshire where his parents now lived. Philip had had a stroke of luck, having found a job as managing director of Walker and Homfrays, a large brewery in Salford, a town close to Manchester.

December 1939. Pedro (never without his pipe)
and fellow sergeant pilot trainees leaving
Cambridge having completed their course at
No. 1 Initial Training Wing. Shortly afterwards
he was commissioned as a pilot officer.

This fortunate appointment – a product of both his brewing and masonic connections – went a long way towards rehabilitating Philip financially, although he was to go on reimbursing the friends who had invested in his ill-starred film venture for another fifteen years.

No. 11 FTS (Tiggy noted with satisfaction the absence of the words reserve and elementary) was tasked with consolidating the flying training already undertaken and preparing its pilots for flying duties with operational squadrons. Here he was re-introduced to the Hart and Audax, picking up the threads of airmanship quickly, but the flying training now was much more intense than that he had so far experienced – he sometimes flew as many as five hours a day so that by the end of June 1940 he had completed over 200 hours in total. Accidents happened and brought home to Tiggy and his fellow trainees that even without an enemy, it was only too easy to be involved in tragedy. One of his friends killed himself by disobeying instructions and crashing while stunt flying too low over the airfield: 'It taught us all a lesson,' he wrote to his mother. 'These planes are the safest ever providing one keeps to the rules of the game. I had been flying in formation with him five minutes before it happened. I had to see his parents and write to tell his girlfriend and I also had to be a pall-bearer at his funeral. All of which was a bit of a strain. They always say these things happen in threes and as there have been three in two weeks, everyone is getting cheerful again!'

Tiggy too had something of a disaster and

recounted his experience to his parents:

'At 2.30 this morning I had a crash while doing solo night-flying. I am all right save for a few bruises. I had taken off for the second time and while circling the aerodrome my cockpit lights shorted and went out so I was left without instruments on a very black night. I decided to try and get down and just before I landed the lights came on again. Unfortunately I paid too much attention to them and misjudged my height and tried to land 50 feet above the ground with the result that I spun those last 50 feet. My right wing hit first and was torn off and then my undercarriage which also came off. Then the propeller and engine were completely smashed and finally I did one and a half somersaults and came to rest upside down. It took a few minutes to get me out as my parachute on which I was sitting was transfixed by a metal bar. Luckily she did not burn. The plane is a wreck and the damage £5,000 but nobody seems to mind much. I think the experience was really a good one as it seemed so humorous at the time. What price Hitler now!

Love,

Tiggy.'

While at Shawbury he saw a lot of his parents, although carefully laid plans to meet had often to be cancelled at the last minute because of the demands of his instructors. He regularly sent money home, not just to buy a birthday present for one of sisters ('here is a postal order for 7/6 for Doddy') but to help Philip and Dodo. At Easter, during which he flew every day and so had to cancel plans to go to Altrincham, he sent his parents a postal order for one pound, adding that 'I should be able to send about £5 the week after next but at the moment I have had to buy a lot of kit'.

At the end of the course he was graded 'average' in all the departments, except for navigation in which he was described, surprisingly, as rather weak – surprisingly because in mid-course he had been singled out for possessing above average navigational skills. He had, however, got his dearest wish by being firmly recommended for fighter training and on the last day of the course received the news that he had been commissioned. He was now Pilot Officer O. V. Hanbury RAFVR.

There followed a frustrating two months as he awaited a place on a fighter conversion course. July was spent at RAF Old Sarum, near Salisbury where he joined No. 1 School of Army Co-operation for four weeks of operational training which involved learning the techniques of spotting for ground artillery, reconnaissance, dive-bombing and aerial photography, as well as the skills of towing drogues for the army's anti-aircraft gunners to shoot at. He was astonished to find that his flight commander was T. M. Longley – the man who had been his immediate boss at the Asiatic Petroleum Company. He was also surprised and gratified to find that his room in the officers' mess was excellent and that the equally acceptable food and drink was delivered by a fleet of Women's Auxiliary Air Force waitresses!

During his time at Old Sarum he flew the Hector, which had replaced the Audax as an army co-operation aircraft, and also the Westland Lysander, the RAF's main liaison and army co-operation aircraft whose short landing and take-off capability from unprepared strips was later to make it famous as the principal carrier for secret agents delivered to and collected from occupied Europe. He became particularly fond of the Lysander but chafed at not yet being allowed to be in the front line as enemy activity over Britain increased, complaining that 'what we do here seems a little like a dead-end as there is at the moment very little army to co-operate with'. He did, however, manage to amuse himself; he wrote to his sister Betty:

'The job means a lot of low-flying at about 50 feet above the ground and 220 miles an hour which gives one a terrific impression of speed. We have to make use of woods and hills to cover our approach and it's rather humorous to see farm labourers prostate themselves as we suddenly appear! We also carry out mock

attacks on convoys of army lorries which gives quite a realistic touch.'

Opportunities for sport were few but he did have one minor triumph: at a cocktail party he met a girl who turned out to be a Lyle ('you know, the sugar-lump kings', he said to his mother) whose family had some trout fishing on the River Wylie. For this Tiggy managed to wangle himself an invitation, wishing only that he had got to know the family earlier.

In August, his course completed, he was off to No. 13 Army Co-operation Squadron stationed at RAF Hooton Park on the Wirral in Cheshire. Once again he was quite near to his parents but once more his anxiety to get to grips with "The Hun" had been frustrated. Although he found most of his fellow pilots 'to be quite a good crowd' Tiggy did not take to Hooton Park. He had to live in a tent and the commanding officer was so disliked as to be generally known as "The Führer" by the rest of the squadron. The work however was quite interesting, conducted mainly over the county of Pembrokeshire in which a great deal of anti-aircraft training was taking place. And then, on 21 August, came the news he had been waiting for:

*'My dear Mummy,
I have been posted to fighters which is great. First I have to go on a conversion course at Hawarden* [near Chester] *and after about a fortnight I will*

*go to a fighter squadron. I believe I shall be
flying Spitfires. Hurrah.*

Love,

Tiggy.'

While Tiggy was preparing enthusiastically for
the action he knew was to come, the news from
Rachel in Hong Kong was far from good. The
Japanese had invaded large chunks of China and
were slowly working their way south. In July
Rachel, in common with all the other wives and
children of servicemen in the colony, had been
packed on to a troop ship and evacuated to the
Philippines as a first stop on the way to a hill-sta-
tion in Burma where eventually Hector was able
to get leave to go and see her.

Tiggy spent barely a week at No. 7 Operational
Training Unit at Hawarden, flying Spitfires for
seventeen hours, practising formation flying,
attack tactics, aerobatics and dog-fighting. On 31
August he met his mother for tea at the Chester
Grosvenor Hotel and three days later he set off for
602 (City of Glasgow) Squadron, Auxiliary Air
Force, at Westhampnett in Sussex. He now had
290 flying hours under his belt.

Chapter Four

THE BATTLE OF BRITAIN – BEWARE THE TORMENTED LION

602 (City of Glasgow) Squadron was formed in September 1925 on the Moorpark aerodrome at Renfrew, the main runway of which has now become a stretch of the M8 near Glasgow Airport. In the 1930s it became a light bomber squadron and, under the command of the Marquess of Douglas and Clydesdale (later the 14th Duke of Hamilton) it moved to Abbotsinch, a mile or so to the west. In 1933 the marquess and his second-in-command, David McIntyre, became the first men to fly over Mount Everest, both being awarded the Air Force Cross and the Freedom of Renfrew.

McIntyre succeeded the marquess in command of 602 and in 1936 King George VI approved the

squadron badge and its motto *Cave Leonem Cruciatum* – Beware the Tormented Lion.

Two years later the squadron, much against the will of both its officers and ground crew, briefly became an army co-operation unit. The marquess and other influential Glasgow families went to work and within two months it had become – as they had all wanted – a fighter squadron, and in May 1939 it was the first of the auxiliaries to be equipped with the Supermarine Spitfire. The characteristic roar of the Rolls-Royce Merlin engine became a familiar sound over the city as the pilots practised their skills. On 23 August, the squadron was called-up and embodied into the RAF in anticipation of the outbreak of war.

In September, 602 and its sister squadron, 603 (City of Edinburgh), moved to Drem airfield in East Lothian and on 16 October 1939 both went into action for the first time, taking on the Junkers Ju88 bombers which had come to attack HMS *Hood* and other shipping in the Firth of Forth. In the first battle of the war to be fought in the skies over the United Kingdom, two enemy aircraft were shot down, one by the joint efforts of Archie McKellar and George Pinkerton of 602 and one by the Edinburgh squadron. There were no British losses. 'Well done. First blood to the Auxiliaries', telegraphed the Commander-in-Chief, Air Chief Marshal Dowding.

In November 1939 the auxiliary squadrons began to receive pilots of the RAFVR and this would increasingly be the pattern as the AAF slowly ceased to retain its original entity. Shortly before the beginning of the Battle of Britain – generally recognised to be 10 July 1940 – Squadron Leader Sandy Johnstone, a pre-war pilot with 602, came to take command, and on 12 August the squadron deployed to Westhampnett, a grass airfield a mile or so from Chichester, and a satellite of the much larger RAF station at nearby Tangmere. There they were to relieve 145 Squadron whose flyers had taken a terrible mauling. As the Spitfires of 602 landed they were greeted by the sight of a burning Hurricane lying on its back and by three of the only four pilots who had survived the battles of the last month. This was to be 602's home for the next four months.

In the late afternoon of 3 September two new officers arrived: Pilot Officers Roy Payne and Osgood Hanbury. They were warmly welcomed by Johnstone, who had been an instructor at Prestwick and knew Tiggy slightly, and (as was invariably the way with the RAF) they were immediately given nicknames. Payne became Agony and Tiggy, because he now affected a carefully cultivated droopy moustache, was henceforth to be known as Pedro; only his family and pre-war friends continued to refer to him as Tiggy.

After a series of tactical briefings and short familiarisation flights during the next two days, Pedro went into action for the first time on the 7th. He was sitting in the officers mess and happened to be nearest to the telephone when it rang sharply. He picked it up and then threw it down shouting 'Scramble, scramble, scramble. Patrol Hawkinge [near Folkestone in Kent]. Angels 15 [shorthand for 15,000 feet].' Johnstone, who was talking to a visitor who happened to be the Chief of the Air Staff, Sir Cyril Newall, hastily excused himself.

Ninety seconds later Hanbury was in the air in N3228, a Supermarine Spitfire Mk1a; he remembered to retract his undercarriage (it was easy to forget – and even easier to forget to lower it again when landing) and checked the firing button which activated the eight .303 inch Browning machine guns mounted in his wings and on which his life now largely depended. His maximum endurance in the air was rather less than one hour.

The squadron, known when airborne by the radio codename Villa, together with twenty other fighter squadrons from all over the south-east of England, had been ordered to intercept enemy raiders attacking London, and its twelve available aircraft took off at 1205. Pedro was flying with two others as Red 3 in the section led by Johnstone who was Red 1. Similar sections of three aircraft were each coded Green, Blue and Yellow. Twenty-eight Dornier Do17 bombers were sighted at 18,000 feet and were seen to be accompanied by an escort of around 100 Messerschmitt Bf109s and Bf110s. What Johnstone had not been able to see when he ordered his squadron into the attack was that three or four further waves of bombers – Heinkel He111s, all escorted by a similar number of fighters – were approaching from the east; around 500 enemy aircraft were crossing the coast and heading for London.

In his book *Lions Rampant*, Douglas McRoberts gives a flavour of the chaos of the battle which followed as he listened to the aircraft radios:

'Jesus, it's the whole of the Luftwaffe.'
'Villa Squadron, aim for the bombers, look out for the snappers *[enemy escort fighters]* coming down. Here they come. Break, break, break.'
'He's a flamer. Jeez that was close.'
'Go for the bombers.......more at two o'clock.'
'Hold on; hold on; I'm coming.'

And then as a portly German floated by on the end of his parachute, his hands held high in surrender:

'Bloody hell, I've shot down Goering.'

Silence for a bit as with his finger frozen on the radio button, a terrified young pilot screamed his agonies to the world. His last seconds lived long with those who heard him.

In this dramatic encounter 602 lost two pilots while claiming three kills and two probable kills in addition to four enemy aircraft damaged.

THE BATTLE OF BRITAIN

Flying Officer Coverley and Pilot Officer Moody died and two further Spitfires were damaged, Hanbury's being one. His radiator had been holed and he was forced to break off from attacking the Dorniers (one of which he had damaged) and make an emergency landing. In a letter home he described his part in the action:

'We flew to Beachy Head at 20,000 feet and then turned towards Tunbridge Wells. Shortly afterwards the commanding officer shouted Tally-ho Villa Squadron and looking around I saw the most amazing sight. There were four or five groups of bombers surrounded by fighters totalling about 500 aircraft. There were only twelve of us as we were the first squadron to attack. We dived down and chose our targets. I went for the middle of the Dorniers and saw my bullets going through one plane and a large lump fell off the engine. I then skimmed over the top but a rear gunner got in a lucky shot and I got one hole in my radiator and another in my right wheel! Smoke and steam poured out so I had to switch off my engine and glide down and was just able to land at West Malling in Kent. A Messerschmitt 109 tried to finish me off but luckily failed. When I got out and was looking around showers of bullets from the fight above started to *whistle about me and I ran like mad to the nearest shelter. Eventually I got back to our place at 2.30 am.*

'It really was a wonderful feeling being able to wade into the Hun like that. I would not miss being down here for anything at the moment and think that everything depends on the next fortnight as he is in dead earnest now.

Must hurry,

Love

Tiggy.'

He became very busy. Two days after his first combat he crashed his Spitfire on landing after a night patrol. He and two others had been sent up at dusk by the wing commander in charge at Tangmere. None of the three had flown a Spitfire at night before and they were told that they would be ordered down before dark. In the event the order to abandon the patrol did not come. Two, including Pedro who over-ran the flare path and finished up in a hedge 'at considerable speed', eventually crash-landed at Tangmere which by that time was under aerial bombardment, and the third had an engine failure and came down on a golf course. The three pilots were uninjured but the aircraft were badly damaged. The offending wing commander was later severely admonished while a squadron leader, held to be responsible for not bringing the Spitfires down in daylight was reduced in rank.

On 12 September, Red Section found a lone Do17 and chased it in and out of clouds all the way to Boulogne. Pedro, having thought that he had managed to 'silence the rear gunner', headed for home but had to land at another airfield to refuel before returning to Westhampnett.

Three days later, Sunday 15 September – now called Battle of Britain Day – the weather dawned fair with cloudy patches but was clear by early evening. There were heavy raids on London but on this day the Luftwaffe suffered its greatest number of casualties for over a month. Pedro, who flew three sorties on that Sunday, was able to contribute his first confirmed kill.

After relating the story of this exciting event to his parents he wrote that the squadron count since it arrived from Drem, now amounted to 'sixty-three Huns for the loss of three pilots killed and about ten wounded – which is a pretty good average'. *[This figure gives a slightly false impression: the total of enemy aircraft confirmed as destroyed by pilots of 602 Squadron by this date was twenty-three. The figure of sixty-three would have included claims of both 'probables' and 'damaged'.]* He added, a little plaintively: 'Thank you for the letters and telegram but I have not yet received my washing. I'm afraid that leave is out of the question until after the blitz.'

For the remainder of September Pedro had a relatively uneventful time until 30 September when the squadron, ten strong, went into action against a dozen Ju88s over Selsey Bill and the Isle of Wight. Later that day he submitted his combat report:

> *'I was Red 2, A Flight. On hearing the CO's command to attack, I picked out a Ju88 in the middle of the formation and made a rear quarter attack for three seconds, closing to about 100 yards, stopping his port engine. He dived below clouds and I followed making attacks from all quarters until I finished my ammunition. Flying in front of him I saw him turn back towards our coast and followed him until he crashed into the sea about half a mile south of Selsey Bill. No survivors. PO Edy confirms seeing the aircraft in the water.'*

This was a most successful engagement by 602 as all the enemy aircraft were turned back without dropping a bomb. Pedro did not mention in his report that he was under fire from the three air-gunners in the Junkers for most of his attack. 'Luckily', he confided later to his mother, 'they were all wide of the mark'.

He tried to see his parents and sisters whenever possible but it was not easy to arrange. It would have taken more time than his occasional 48-hour rest periods allowed to travel to Cheshire so that once or twice Philip and Dodo came to Sussex, staying a little further inland (and therefore, in theory more safely) than in Chichester. The difficulty inherent in making plans for a visit, apart from the problems of wartime travel, was that Pedro never knew when his next break would be, but somehow they seem to have managed. Philippa, who was doing war work in Scotland and, after his parents was his most constant correspondent, sent him a box of Edinburgh Rock which he shared with the other pilots: 'It all went in a flash', he reported.

On 5 October Pedro came very close to death. He had chased a Ju88 reconnaissance aircraft in and out of clouds as it ran for France. He had tried several attacks from the rear but knew that Junkers configured to fly without a bomb load were heavily armour-plated and difficult to bring down, especially from behind. He therefore overtook the enemy and when about 1,100 yards ahead turned to confront him head-on. He put the Junkers starboard engine out of commission and was preparing to attack again when he noticed that he was over Boulogne and only 6,000 feet up – well within range of German anti-aircraft guns. He also saw three blobs in the distance which turned out to be Bf109s closing fast. Prudently Pedro turned for home, but this manoeuvre brought him face to face with the enemy fighters. As the range decreased he pressed his firing button; there was a pop of tracer and then silence, he had expended his ammunition. Luckily the few tracer bullets had been enough to cause the Messerschmitts to turn away briefly and Pedro climbed for the nearest clouds. He had, he wrote to his parents, never been so frightened in all his life. He had 70 miles to run and each time he emerged briefly into clear sky he saw the enemy still on his tail, swooping and searching. As he reached the English coast he dived to sea level and lost them. 'I think', he finished his letter, 'this was really my most exciting trip as it lasted longer than the other combats I have had'.

His parents came down on Friday the 17th and there was some speculation that Doddy and Betty – both driving ambulances at different ends of the country – would come too. In the event neither was able to make it. At the end of the month he had a 48-hour break which he spent in London, staying at the Cumberland Hotel in Marble Arch, inspecting the bomb damage, collecting some luggage from the Lensbury Club and visiting Gieves, his tailor. He was, he reported to his parents, astonished that, in the hotel, when the whistling of a bomb was heard, all the guests immediately lay on the floor – 'even little old ladies' – and then got up again without looking in the least bit self-conscious. His pleasure at this short holiday was entirely eroded by the news that 602 had not only been in action in his absence but had had their most successful battle so far. On 29 October the squadron, led by Flight Lieutenant Mickey Mount, an Old Etonian, was scrambled and climbed towards London. With four other squadrons – two Spitfire and two Hurricane – a trap was laid for a Messerschmitt force which had earlier been sighted. 602 was in the thick of it, diving to attack from 30,000 feet. Its pilots were credited with eight confirmed kills and one probable for the loss of no one and with only one

LO-J (X4162) was a Spitfire of 602 (City of Glasgow) Squadron Royal Auxiliary Air Force flown by Pedro from RAF Westhampnett in the Battle of Britain from September 1940. In it, on 30 October 1940 (the eve of the last official day of the Battle of Britain), he destroyed a Messerschmitt Bf109 over Dungeness.

Spitfire slightly damaged. Pedro, reading about this in the morning paper as he returned from London by train, professed himself 'green with envy'.

He was back for lunch and that same afternoon he had his moment. He was one of nine who took off to intercept forty Bf109s over Dungeness and the sea. To begin with the Messerschmitts had the advantage of height and 602 became split up as the dog-fighting began. Pedro, while making a climbing beam attack, stalled and entered inadvertently into a spin. Recovering, he climbed again to 30,000 feet and rejoined the fray, taking on three of the enemy who were trying to make it to a circle of safety. He fired at one which burst into flames, its pilot ejecting. He was then forced to break away with two enemy on his tail. The squadron had had another successful engagement, destroying two Messerschmitts, while losing only two aircraft; both Spitfire pilots, however, survived – one with a piece of shrapnel in his bottom!

The following day marked the official end of the Battle of Britain – although many pilots, including those of 602 Squadron, believed it continued into 1941. Pilot Officer Hanbury now had three kills to his credit (one Bf109; one Bf110 and one Ju88) with a further Ju88 shared. He had severely damaged three other enemy aircraft – two Do17s and one Ju88. The City of Glasgow Squadron remained at Westhampnett until 17 December and during that seven weeks, Pedro was airborne on twenty-nine separate days, flying for thirty-four hours. Enemy aircraft, however, were few and far between and only once was he in combat, sadly witnessing the death of his friend Pat Lyall.

Even though he was now a section leader, the lack of Germans meant that he had more time for sporting activities. He had managed to acquire a stalking rifle and with this he took a surprising toll of the Duke of Richmond and Gordon's game as he ranged the Goodwood estate of which the airfield was part. His bag for November and early December amounted to thirty-seven pheasants, two hares, six partridges, one pigeon and two rabbits. Despite this poaching (or perhaps because of it) he was invited to join a local, law-abiding shooting syndicate and sent post-haste for his shotgun. 'Makes a change from roast beef', he wrote to his father.

The squadron's journey north to its home base at Prestwick was broken to refuel at RAF Catterick in Yorkshire where Johnstone, who had not warned Catterick that they were coming, was surprised to find that not only were the fuel bowsers waiting, but vehicles were standing-by to take them all to the mess for lunch. They had just finished an excellent meal when the roar of Spitfires landing took them to the windows. It was 603 (City of Edinburgh) Squadron; the lunch had been laid on for them!

Glasgow was pleased to see its own squadron back again after such a distinguished tour (during its time at Westhampnett it had claimed a total of thirty-five and a half kills for the loss of fifteen aircraft) so that civic receptions and other parties abounded. There was, however, no action until Thursday 13 March 1941 when Clydeside and Glasgow were blitzed for the first time. Pedro and his close friend, Nigel Rose, were among four Spitfires of 602 which, together with a number of Blenheim and Beaufighter specialist nightfighters, were ordered to undertake a Fighter Night. This was a tactic whereby fighters patrolled the skies above Glasgow at varying heights (in this case 14,000 feet upwards) while the city's anti-aircraft defences would have free rein at targets up to 12,000 feet. Rose, in a letter to his parents, reported that there was some difficulty in picking out Glasgow itself from the thousands of incendiaries which had already been dropped: large areas of Clydeside were brightly lit and here and there was the ugly dark red of a fire burning fiercely.

Pedro's was the highest aircraft of the four from 602 and, at 24,000 feet, a couple of thousand feet above Rose. He glimpsed and chased a Ju88, firing 960 rounds at it, but much to his irritation, inconclusively, although an unclaimed bomber fell into the docks which he felt might well have been his doing. The Spitfires didn't land until well after midnight and Rose, to whom Pedro had lent his car to help his friend make arrangements for his forthcoming wedding, was relieved when fog prevented them from resuming patrols the following night. There was, however, no leave for Pedro. He explained to his parents that all the 'old stagers' except five, of which he was accounted one, had been posted to other squadrons and there were lots of new pilots to be trained and also 'for three weeks out of four (when there is a bit of a moon), we have to fly at night for the protection of Glasgow'.

In April, 602 Squadron was deployed for a short time to RAF Heathfield near Ayr during which it had no excitements in the air. There were, however, plenty of opportunities for high jinks on the ground. One late evening two fires broke out in the officers' mess in the Old Mill as a party, including Hanbury, celebrated boisterously the good fortune of one of their number who was to be posted. In the ensuing excitement Pedro unwisely discharged a fire extinguisher over the station's chief flying instructor. Together with two others he was placed under close arrest and the police were called. The next day, Scottish Aviation, the owners of Prestwick, announced their intention of evicting the officers from the Old Mill to prevent further damage. The Duke of Hamilton was informed and managed both to deflect Scottish Aviation's desire for revenge and have the alleged miscreants released to be dealt with summarily by the station commander. The fire was later found to have been started by an arsonist who had already burnt down some buildings on the other side of the airfield.

Pedro now began to thirst for more orthodox excitement and when his friend Mickey Mount was tasked with taking 260 Squadron, equipped with Hurricanes, to the Middle East, Pedro eagerly volunteered to join him. His last flight with 602 took place on 4 May on a routine patrol. A week later he was flying Hurricanes at Drem where 260 was forming up.

Chapter Five

WAR IN THE DESERT – SWIFT AND STRONG

260 Squadron RAF had been formed at Westward Ho! in Devon in August 1918. Its short incarnation ended only six months later when it was disbanded. On 22 November 1940 at Castletown, close to Wick in Caithness, 260 was reformed with Hurricanes and flew on air defence and convoy patrols with special responsibility for the naval base at Scapa Flow in the Orkneys. From there it moved to Drem to begin preparations for the transfer to the Middle East.

Its motto, incorporated below the squadron's badge, was *Celer et Fortis,* Swift and Strong, and it was to live up to this noble aspiration more than once in the years to come. Squadron Leader C.J.

(Mickey) Mount DFC (later to become Air Commodore Mount CBE DSO DFC) was four years older than Pedro, so although their time at Eton had briefly overlapped, their schoolboy paths had never crossed. Mount, like his young colleague from 602, thirsted for a little more action than was apparently to be their lot now that the Luftwaffe threat to the freedom of the skies over the United Kingdom had largely receded.

In an operation codenamed WS-8B by the Admiralty, the pilots and Hurricanes of 260 were separated from their ground crews – the practice being to send the latter to the Middle East by civilian ship routed round the Cape of Good Hope and up to East Africa (usually Kenya) whence they would be airlifted to Egypt. The pilots and aircraft, however, were to embark at Scapa Flow on to the aircraft carrier *HMS Victorious* which would carry them to Gibraltar in the first of several legs of a voyage by sea and air.

Shortly before he boarded Tiggy wrote to his parents giving them an army post office address, adding elliptically: 'I am afraid I can't use the code we arranged as this operation is extremely secret and you must not mention to anyone the possible method I suggested.' This was, perhaps, just as well as *Victorious* instead of heading south sailed out into the North Atlantic, together with the battleship HMS *King George V*, the battle-cruiser *Repulse* and four light cruisers to join the hunt for the German battleship *Bismarck*. In what Tiggy later described as 'a pretty exciting chase' *Bismarck* was attacked – without any damaging effect – by nine torpedo-launching Swordfish bi-planes (known as string-bags in the navy) from *Victorious*, but was eventually cornered by the task force and sunk on 27 May. *Victorious* now turned her bows to the south, the plan being that at Gibraltar 260 Squadron would be transferred to another carrier which would take them into the Mediterranean to a point some halfway to Malta at which the Hurricanes would fly off the carriers, land at Malta and then prepare for an onward flight to North Africa.

The trip to Gibraltar was uneventful and there the squadron was transhipped to HMS *Ark Royal*, which had also been involved in the *Bismarck* battles and which under more normal circumstances was the only carrier allotted to Force H, the naval task force charged with controlling the western Mediterranean. On this occasion, however, HMS *Victorious* was to join her – *Ark Royal* embarking the twenty Hurricanes of 260 while *Victorious* retained on board twenty-eight belonging to 238 Squadron, also bound for North Africa. Pedro and his fellow pilots were now in for a rough time.

On 14 June and approximately 600 miles east of Gibraltar, four Hudson aircraft from Malta circled overhead. Their task was to guide twelve Hurricanes each, safely on their next leg. Two

Hurricanes – both belonging to 238 Squadron – were immediately in trouble: one failed to take off at all and one almost immediately developed engine trouble and was last seen heading for the African coast. Pedro and his colleagues were led by a Hudson pilot who first missed Malta to the north and, after turning south, missed the island again by about ten miles. Eventually they found their objective but by that time, having been in the air for over six hours, the Hurricanes were very short of fuel. One ran out completely and ditched in the sea from where the pilot, Sergeant Saunders, was eventually rescued, but another, also out of fuel, went into a spin over the island and crash-landed. The pilot was killed.

After an investigation initiated by a furious Mickey Mount and the commander of 238 Squadron, it appeared that all four Hudsons had been flown by inexperienced crews – some on their first operational flight. A report to the Air Ministry said (of the Hudson escorting the ill-fated aircraft of 260) that its crew was incapable of looking after itself, much less escort twelve Hurricanes. The Hudson pilot was placed under arrest. Over the next two days the remainder of 260 flew to Mersah Matruh, an RAF station on the north coast of Egypt some 200 miles west of Alexandria. They landed after the four-hour flight only to refuel, and were soon on their way to RAF Abu Sueir, some ten miles west of Ismailia. There the squadron met up with the ground crews of 450 Squadron, Royal Australian Air Force who were to look after them for the foreseeable future.

450 Squadron, and its sister 451, had been formed in Sydney the previous February as 'infiltration squadrons' – that is consisting only of ground crews whose aircraft would catch up with them in the Middle East once enough pilots were fully trained. Meanwhile they amalgamated with 260 Squadron under the joint leadership of Mickey Mount and Squadron Leader Gordon Steege RAAF. On 20 June 1941, 260/450 began to deploy to Palestine, split between two RAF airfields, one at Aqir (fifteen miles south of Tel Aviv) and the other at Haifa. Their mission was to support the allied invasion of Vichy French-controlled Syria and Lebanon. This action, known as Operation Exporter, was fought on the ground largely by Australian and Indian divisions supported by two Free French brigades who were opposed by seven Vichy battalions supported by some Lebanese and Syrian units.

In the air, RAF and RAAF fighter aircraft were initially outnumbered by those of the Vichy forces but the imbalance was corrected early as the enemy lost large numbers of aircraft on the ground where they were carelessly parked out in the open unprotected against attacks from the air.

On 23 June, 260 Squadron was in action, shooting up the Syrian airfield at Baalbeck, destroying both a Ju52 and a number of French aircraft. Pedro became separated from the rest and, on his way to base, was attacked by three Vichy aircraft (probably Dewoitine D520 fighters) which he failed to recognise as enemy until it was almost too late. He was hit in the arm and shoulder, but managed to reach Haifa and landed safely. During his subsequent spell in hospital he was to note ruefully in his log-book that: 'My aircraft recognition should be polished up!' As he was about to return to his squadron in July he wrote home with a full account of his adventure:

'I come out of hospital tomorrow having spent a dull three weeks under the auspices of the Army. I shall probably rejoin my squadron and stay on ground duties for a week or two and then go back to flying. My arm feels pretty good although rather weak as is natural. It [the bullet] *has left an inconspicuous scar and with any luck it will never trouble me again.*

'Now that the Syria campaign is over, I think it safe to say that it was in that which I was wounded. It fell to me to lead an attack on a Vichy aerodrome where we strafed their aircraft on the ground. That lasted a few minutes and was great fun and successful. But on the way back I got caught by three Vichy fighters who had me completely at their mercy as I had no ammunition left. Their shooting was pretty bad as they used up all their ammo (about 4,000 to 5,000 rounds) and there were only thirty holes in my machine. Five came through the cockpit of which one hit and another grazed me. The time they hit me was when they came one on each side

and one behind me while I was signalling them to come into formation with me and it was not until they fired that I realised that they weren't British planes!

'After that we had the most violent chase round in small circles over the sea near Beirut and at one time I thought I was finished. I tried to bale out but fell back in again. After they had finished all their ammo they left me and I was able to creep down the coast with very little petrol left and a very sore back and arm. However I made it without further event and managed to land with my left hand. I must say it was a very unpleasant experience and I only wish I had been able to get another crack at the Frenchies before they packed up.'

The war on the ground lasted only a few weeks and in the air an attack by American-built Tomahawk fighters of 3 Squadron RAAF on Homs airfield in Syria on 26 June, during which they put eleven enemy aircraft out of action in a few seconds, virtually put an end to resistance, although patrols continued from both Haifa and Aqir until mid-August. There followed a period of relative inactivity taken up with largely routine and unopposed air defence patrolling of the skies over Palestine, Lebanon and Syria. 260 Squadron's ground crews now arrived and those of 450 left for North Africa after a most amicable partnership. But although reunited as a squadron, elements of 260 were based not only at Haifa and

Aqir but also at El Bassa on the Lebanese border.

Pedro was quickly bored by inactivity, even wishing occasionally that he had never volunteered for the Middle East. Living conditions during July, August and September were however, very agreeable: at El Bassa his flight was camped in an olive grove surrounded by fruit trees of practically every variety and they had the warm Mediterranean Sea in which to bathe. His shoulder had mended well and in the moments when he was not fretting about the lack of action, he mused that he had begun to feel that after the war he might like to make his career in the RAF.

On 26 August, he wrote to his friend Nigel Rose, still with 602 Squadron in Scotland:

> *'Dear Rosebud,*
> *Just a line. Mickey* [Mount] *and I are in the land of milk and honey. He had a very severe attack of peritonitis and is in hospital but I am fighting fit. Do write and tell me all the squadron news.*
>
> *'This is a pretty lousy country and I can't think what madness took me from 602! Have had very little excitement apart from an early dust-up in the Syria/Lebanon show which ended with me in hospital. Well all the best and do write some time.*
> *Yours,*
>
> *Pedro.'*

This is not exactly informative – even by wartime

standards when very little escaped the eye of the censors. But it is evident from his log-book that the only flying he did – some ten hours in late August and only nineteen in the whole of September – was in practice or training. Only once in six weeks was there any reference to the enemy, when one night an unidentified aircraft dropped an incendiary on Haifa; this prolonged inaction was not at all what he expected when volunteering for service in the Middle East.

In the first half of October he was sent to Egypt on a course and then had a few days leave in Cairo (where he stayed at Shepherd's Hotel and explored the pyramids) and Alexandria where, quite by chance, he met his Creek Crawlers friend, Charles Coles, and spent some time in trying to arrange a duty-free shipment of silk stockings and other goodies from South Africa for his mother and sisters as Christmas presents. Then came the good news – 260 Squadron was to deploy to the Western Desert; there was every prospect at last of Pedro again coming to grips with the Hun he had come to hate.

The squadron was now under the command of Squadron Leader Derek Walker, a tough, aggressive twenty-six year old from south London – about as far removed in terms of background from Mickey Mount (or indeed Pedro Hanbury) as it would be possible to be. From the start though, he was to prove an inspiring leader and he had one other great advantage – he was such an accomplished pianist that the squadron officers 'liberated' the piano from the mess at El

Bassa and somehow carted it all the way into the desert. Walker's favourite song, according to the Australian pilot, Sergeant Ron Cundy, was 'If Your Engine Cuts Out You'll Have No Balls At All' – a reference to one of the more unsavoury habits of desert Bedouin women! There were other newcomers too: two Canadian pilots, Sergeants Jimmy Price and Joe Bernier had arrived, together with a draft of Royal Canadian Air Force (RCAF) ground crew.

First stop was the huge RAF base at Kasfareet on the west coast of the Great Bitter Lake stretch of the Suez Canal where two days were spent on maintenance while pilots and ground crew alike celebrated Pedro's promotion to the rank of flying officer. The next move was to Edku (sometimes spelt Idku) on the coast twenty miles east of Alexandria, and then west again to Landing Ground (LG) 102, inland between Fuka and Mersah Matruh. A succession of westward moves followed, ending at LG 124 at Fort Maddalena in Libya just over the Egyptian border and deep in the desert fifty miles south of Sollum.

Maddalena was little more than a salt flat; pilots and ground crews lived in tents – most no better or bigger than bivouacs – while mess tents for all ranks were rickety marquees known as EPIPs (European Personnel Indian Pattern) which by their very nature were prone to being brought down by the frequent sand storms. The commanding officer's combined office and living quarters was a caravan trailer while the all-important communications equipment was housed in similar vehicles.

260 Squadron's pilots' mess tent which accompanied them throughout the desert campaign. Their name, European Personnel Indian Pattern, gives a clue to their origin; in these tents the pilots ate and were briefed.

Maintenance equipment, spare parts, ammunition and all the other necessities of war were stored in vehicles so that the squadron base could move quickly in an emergency. Slit trenches were sited alongside the accommodation and mess tents as well as the vehicles and trailers to give some protection against bombing and strafing raids.

Water was carried in old petrol barrels and was impossible to drink without first being boiled, and the daily diet was an almost unremitting combination of corned (bully) beef and biscuits, supplemented very occasionally by fresh rations, either issued officially or in the form of game shot by Pedro and his like-minded colleagues. It was a life almost entirely devoid of comfort.

260 Squadron was now part of 262 (Fighter) Wing, the other components of which at this time were three Tomahawk squadrons (two of them RAF and one from the South African Air Force, the SAAF), together with three Hurricane squadrons. The wing's principal operational roles were those of escorting bombers and patrolling offensively as, on the ground, the advance west-wards of the British 8th Army's under the code-name Operation Crusader got underway. The objective of Crusader was the relief of the key port of Tobruk, which had been under siege by Rommel's Afrika Korps and its Italian allies since April. The loss of Tobruk to the Axis forces would have crucially shortened Rommel's supply lines.

On 13 November, shortly before offensive patrolling began in earnest, Pedro wrote to Patricia Harman. Few letters of his to her now exist before this date (and none from her to him) but it is clear that their courtship, which had con-tinued on and off, for about four years, was reach-ing a satisfactory conclusion:

> *My darling Patricia,*
> *Just a quick line to say that all's well. Have had a few letters from you lately. Am glad to hear it will probably be "Yes"! Well, darling, it won't be long now before I am home again and*

the war is over. It is very cold at night here but just right during the day time.

'I hope the shoot keeps the larder full this winter. Saw some geese the other day. Would be interested to hear what William's job in the RAF is.

With all my love, darling,

your Tiggy

XXX.'

He had, it seems, proposed marriage and had been given very high hopes by her reply. At this time Patricia had been living for some months at a house called Gortinane in the village of Tayinloan in Argyll on the west coast of Kintyre, the home of Douglas Speed and his wife. The Speeds had lived in Kent, where Douglas had been master of the East Kent and West Street Foxhounds from 1935 to 1937, and become firm friends of the Hanburys, but had then moved to Gortinane where Douglas played a major role in the Home Guard, employing Patricia as his driver. The William mentioned by Tiggy was Patricia's brother who had joined the RAF as a technician, having trained to be an electrical engineer at Faraday House in London. He was later to transfer to the Royal Electrical and Mechanical Engineers – an army unit.

On 18 November, 260 Squadron was patrolling over the 8th Army's advancing tanks when it was

Left: Tiggy's father, Philip Hanbury, in the uniform of a senior lieutenant of the Yorkshire Regiment, at the regimental depot in Richmond in early 1915. He was soon to be in the trenches and, as a captain, commanding C Company of the 2nd Battalion.

t: Dorothy Maude (Dodo) rgary in Ceylon (now Sri ka) in 1905 when she was eteen. Dodo was the ngest of the seven children a tea planter, Henry rgary and his wife, herine. She married Philip bury in 1913.

Above left: Philip Hanbury (1802-1 was the fifth son of Osgood Susannah (neé Barclay) and follo his father into Barnett, Ho Hanbury and Lloyd, bankers London. He married Elizabeth C d'Escury, daughter of a Dutch b and lived in Redhill in Surrey. He Tiggy's great grandfather.

Above: Captain Philip Hanbury, 1917-1918. For most of the last years of the First World War he found unfit for active service, st ing from persistent bronchitis occasional pneumonia. During time he was a successful commar of a musketry school near Darlir and adjutant of his regiment's Battalion in Richmond.

Left: Philip Hanbury, Tiggy's fa fishing the North Esk river in Sco in the late 1930s. At this time he Dodo were living in Altrinc Cheshire, while he was mana director of the brewery Walker Homfrays in Salford.

Top: Presentation of new colours to the 1st Battalion Royal Sussex by HRH The Duke of Gloucester at Chichester in 1928. Lieutenant Colonel Charles Harman here commanding the 1st Battalion, is second from the left and slightly behind the Duke.

Above: The Meath foxhounds in the closing years of the nineteenth century. On his feet is William Harman of Crossdrum, near Oldcastle who was Charles Harman's father and Patricia's grandfather.

Lt. Colonel Charles Cecil
ry DSO and Bar. His military
began in the Leinster Regiment
hom he served in India, South
and during WWI. When most of
sh regiments were disbanded in
e joined the Royal Sussex which
t on to command.

Top left: Mrs Philip Hanbury (Tiggy's mother her eldest child, Rachel, born in 1915.

Top right: Tiggy aged about eighteen months garden of Mote Hall, Bearstead, near Maidst Kent at a time when his father, newly demob began work at the family brewery, Jude Han

Above left: Tiggy whilst at Wellesley Preparatory School in 1928. He was a keen, very accomplished, cricketer both at We House and at Eton. The family had a private et ground at Updown House, Eastry, in Ken

Left: Tiggy, aged eight, on the sands at San Bay, only a few miles away from the family Updown House. He and his sisters spent happy days at Sandwich which boasted su tial dunes.

ove: Dodo Hanbury and her chil-
en in 1926. From left, the chil-
en are: Doddy (aged five),
hilippa (eighteen months), Tiggy
ine), Rachel (eleven) and Betty
even).

Below: The Hanbury family at
Altrincham, Cheshire in 1939.
From left to right: Philip, Betty,
Tiggy, Doddy, Philippa and
Patricia. Rachel, the eldest was in
Hong Kong and was married to
Captain Henry (Hector) Harland
of the Royal Scots.

Top left: Tiggy's leaving photograph at Eton. He was at Eton from September 1930 to July 1935. According to family legend he was required to leave early because of a misdemeanour concerning a girl and a London nightclub, but sadly the school has no record of this!

Bottom Left: A happy Tiggy, aged nineteen, going native in Bavaria. In April 1936, after a few weeks in France the previous year, he went to Germany to learn the language.

Top right: Boys cricket at Upd[own] House in the summer of 1927; Tig[gy] standing, second from the left. He [was] a hugely enthusiastic cricketer [and] never lost an opportunity for a g[ame] One of his team appears to be mis[sing]

Bottom right: A meet of the A[...] Beagles at Updown House in 193[6] before Tiggy's departure for Ger[many] He is on the extreme right. Second [from] the left is Henry (Hector) Harland [who] was to marry Tiggy's eldest s[ister] Rachel, two years later in Hong K[ong]

t: The course at No. 1 Initial Training ; featured emergency first aid. ant Pilot Hanbury and comrades in November 1939 with what seems fire-fighting equipment.

n left: August 1940, No. 7 ational Training Wing at RAF rden. There for barely a week, he seventeen hours before getting s to report to 602 Squadron. Within posing for this photograph he was n the Battle of Britain.

Top right: Sergeant Pilot O.V. Hanbury poses for the camera while on a course at No. 11 Flying Training School at RAF Shawbury near Shrewsbury in early 1940.

Bottom right: This is a portrait of Pedro taken in Chichester (near Westhampnett) in September 1940 for the benefit of Patricia Harman and his parents a few days after he acquired his RAF soubriquet from the pilots of 602 Squadron.

Above: The pilots of 602 Squadron Royal Auxiliary Air Force, Westhampnett in late 1940 at the height of the Battle of Britain. Pedro is seated left on the ground.

Right, middle and bottom: Spitfire X4382 at RAF Westhampnett in late 1940. In the first, Pedro strokes the propeller affectionately. Pilots developed a superstitious affinity with an individual aircraft, particularly one which got them home safely as this aircraft did when Pedro was ambushed by three Messerschmitt Bf109s while almost over Boulogne on 5 October 1940. Pedro flew this aircraft while destroying two enemy aircraft on his own account, plus one shared with another pilot. He had severely damaged three further enemy aircraft. X4382 survived the war.

Above: Pilots of 602 Squadron at RAF Westhampnett, October 1940. Pedro is on the far right, clutching his omnipresent pipe, and rather more solemn than his comrades.

Left: 260 Squadron pilots in September 1942. Front left is Flt Sgt Eddie Edwards, RCAF and next to him is Flt Ron Cundy, RAAF — two of the most successful pilots in the Desert Air Force.

Bottom: A gathering of commanders at Gasr el Arid, June 1942. From left: Wg Cdr Barney Beresford, leader of 233 Wing and future godfather to Pedro's son Christopher. Sqn Ldr Billy Drake (112 Squadron), Flight Lieutenant Willy Williams (450 Squadron) and Pedro.

Above: Pedro with Flt Lt Ron Cundy of the Royal Australian Air Force. Alongside Flt Lt Eddie Edwards of the Royal Canadian Air Force, Ron Cundy was one of 260 Squadron's top pilots. He left 260 Squadron at the beginning of 1943 to sail home to Australia to defend his homeland against Japanese air attack.

Left: Pedro in the desert while in command of 260 Squadron; *Below:* Perhaps writing one of his many letters home.

Top: Four Kittyhawk:
the desert. The squad
tactical formation wa
ally broken down
flights of four or eig
craft.

Middle: The Kittyhaw
X, with which
destroyed a Messersc
Bf 109 over Churgia
January 1943.

Above: The Delta Lily. This was a captured twin-engine Heinkel 111 abandoned
retreating Luftwaffe on the ground at Derna together with a spare engine and,
ingly, a technical handbook. It was in good condition and Pedro had it repain
260 Squadron livery. Initially flown by Ron Cundy, it proved invaluable for c
ing supplies from Alexandria and ferrying off-duty pilots for a night out.

Top: Pedro (seated centre with folded arms) and the aircrew of 260 Squadron, shortly after his promotion to squadron leader at Gambut in April 1942. Pedro had just heard that he was to be awarded a Distinguished Flying Cross (DFC).

Above: Pedro in pensive mood, February 1943.

Left: The grave of Sergeant John Colley RAF, a 260 Squadron pilot killed on 10 March 1943 while attacking targets in Tunisia.

Squadron Leader and Mrs Osgood
ers Hanbury, Saturday, 22 May 1943.

The wedding party at Chailey Moat,
rday 22 May 1943. Behind Tiggy is his
er Philip Hanbury and next to Patricia
er father, Charlie Harman. Dodo
bury (Tiggy's mother) is seated left
Patricia's mother, Muriel Harman, is
ed right. The best man (in uniform next
hilip) is Patricia's brother, William.

e *left:* Tiggy and Patricia with their best
, William Harman in the uniform of
newly formed Royal Electrical and
hanical Engineers, and unknown
esmaid.

Above right: Tiggy (Pedro was always Tiggy
to his family) and Patricia on honeymoon
at Chailey Moat, 1 June 1943. On the way
to the departure airport for a flight back to
the desert, his vehicle broke down and he
was able to snatch a further forty-eight
hours with Patricia.

Above: Pilots of Luftwaffe un
Staffel/Kampfgeschwader.
from the left is Leutnant I
Olbrecht who, flying a Ju
fighter Ju88C-6 over the B.
Biscay, on 3 June 1943, shot
the Hudson aircraft in v
Pedro was travelling back to I
Africa. None of the crew or
sengers of the Hudson were
seen again.

Left: Squadron Leader Osgo
Villiers Hanbury DSO DFC
Bar, taken shortly before
wedding in May 1943. He v
twenty-six years old.

enveloped in a sandstorm and forced to land, remaining on the ground for several hours. When they returned to base, there was news of an Axis counter-attack which made it necessary for the squadron to move east to LG 109.

The remaining days of the month saw intense air activity, Pedro flying over thirty hours in ten days, most of them in escorting and covering Blenheim bombers targeting enemy routes, air-fields and supply lines as the tank battles swayed fro and to. During this time the squadron lost an experienced pilot, Flying Officer John Wyley RAF, who failed to return from one of the sorties.

Early in December the squadron moved to Sidi Rezegh deep in the desert twenty miles south-east of Tobruk and the scene of fierce tank battles in November. Axis air activity had by now, however, lessened because of a shortage of fuel – a mark of the importance of denying them the port of Tobruk.

On 13 December, Derek Walker was wounded while escorting Blenheims attacking Martuba air-field. Although managing to land safely back at base, he had to be rushed to hospital and was eventually sent back to England being replaced by Squadron Leader T.B. (Barney) de la Poer Beresford.

The next day Pedro embarked on an expedition which curiously had become known as a 'rhubarb'. This was not a tactic universally approved of and involved two aircraft flying underneath low cloud over enemy territory and shooting up any target that presented itself, planning to climb quickly into the safety of the cloud if intercepted. Rhubarbing was always risky and sometimes disastrous, but this particular sortie took him westwards from Gazala, where he met and destroyed a Ju88 over Tmimi and damaged a Bf109. Sadly, on the same day, Flight Lieutenant Harry Bandinell, a former Battle of Britain pilot, failed to return.

On 18 December the squadron advanced westwards once more – this time to one of three landing grounds on the coast at Gazala – they were now west of Tobruk. Pedro though was not with them. For a few days he had been feeling unwell and the medical officer diagnosed a serious case of jaundice. He was evacuated to the military hospital in Alexandria and there he was to stay under treatment until sent on recuperation leave to Cairo where he again saw Charles Coles.

He was away from the squadron until the end of January, during which time came the news that Hong Kong had fallen and that his brother-in-law, Hector, had been taken prisoner by the Japanese; there was to be no further news of him for years. Rachel, meanwhile, had been evacuated again – this time from Burma, where she had given birth to a daughter, Henrietta – to Ootacamund, a hill station in southern India where she was to spend the rest of the war. Tiggy had been asked to be Henrietta's godfather.

While Pedro was on leave 260 Squadron heard that it was to re-equip with the American designed and built Kittyhawk fighter. The allied pilots in the desert regarded the Kittyhawk with mixed feelings. Certainly it was quicker and faster than the Hurricane in the dive but it was markedly less manoeuvrable. It was no match for the Messerschmitt Bf109 either in speed, rate of climb or height, but it did possess six wing-mounted .50inch machine guns which proved excellent for strafing and blowing up targets on the ground. In a dog-fight, however, there was an alarming tendency for the guns to stop firing suddenly as excessive 'G' forces came into play.

What the pilots of the Desert Air Force really yearned for was the Spitfire, and they could not help wondering (often out loud to the discomfort of senior officers) why so many Spitfires, the most superior fighter of all, were – as they saw it – languishing in the United Kingdom when the real action was in North Africa. Morale, however, remained high and the, by now, multi-national flyers of 260 Squadron were confident that, even with the Kittyhawk Mark I, they could take on and beat whatever the Luftwaffe could throw at them. Sadly this optimism was not always justified, particularly when Bf109s, lurking at high altitude swooped down at unmatchable speeds.

Training for the conversion of the pilots was carried out on the Tomahawk, an earlier version of the Kittyhawk, and this went on from February until mid-March 1942 from LGs 101 and 115, south-east of Mersah Matruh and well away from the front line. On 13 March the squadron, now part of a newly formed 233 (Fighter) Wing together with 2 and 4 Squadrons SAAF and 94 Squadron RAF, deployed to Gasr el Arid some twenty-five miles west of Bardia. Pedro, promoted to flight lieutenant, took over B Flight of 260 from Flight Lieutenant Hall who had been repatriated for reasons of ill health.

With promotion came a welcome pay-rise of ten shillings a day which, he confided to his parents, would enable him to pay off an outstanding debt of £50 to his Aunt Kitty (Lady Hadow): 'As far as I can calculate I should now have £60 in the bank but daren't write a cheque until I get a statement!'

Offensive patrolling now started in earnest, as did the squadron's other role of providing protection for bombers. On the 20th twelve Kittyhawks accompanied half-a-dozen Boston bombers flown by the SAAF whose mission was to attack the German-held airfield at Martuba. The Kittyhawks were engaged by Bf109s and lost four aircraft, three of them, however, landing safely. Flight Sergeant Tom Hindle managed to shoot down one of three Messerschmitts attacking him and landed without further incident at El Adem. Most importantly, none of the bombers were lost. Flight Sergeant Ron Cundy RAAF recorded this mission as one that had 'bags of twitch', a term for which a polite translation would be extreme buttock-clenching; the "Ring Twitchers Club" had a considerable membership among the aircrews of the Western Desert!

On the last day of March, Barney Beresford was posted to take command of 233 Wing and Pedro was promoted to acting squadron leader to command 260. His delight was evident in a letter home:

> '*I have got command and am now a squadron leader (acting of course!). Wonders will never cease. We are very busy just now and I am very fit and full of life. I have an excellent set of fellows in my squadron.*'

One of those 'excellent fellows' was Flight Sergeant J.F. (Eddie) Edwards, Royal Canadian Air Force, who recalled his first impressions of Pedro when he joined 260 after the withdrawal from frontline duties of his previous unit:

> '*He was reserved, cool and quiet and had a knack of dealing with his pilots. He was steely-grey, a real ex-Battle of Britain character. Discipline became paramount in the air and his combat experience taught younger comrades a great deal. Hanbury did not tolerate line-shooting among his boys, so when victories over enemy aircraft were allowed and confirmed they were – for most of them – easy to corroborate from enemy records.*'

This from a young Canadian, whose judgement on his British boss was fully shared by the other Canadians and the Australian pilots of 260, was a compliment indeed. Young pilots from the Dominions, often brought up in a more informal

A line of 260 Squadron's Kittyhawks sitting in
the desert at Gambut. Nearest the camera is
HS-X, the aircraft in which Pedro shot down a
Junkers JU87 and an Italian MC202 on 25
April 1942. Next to it is HS-B, usually flown
by Eddie Edwards.

environment than their British counterparts, were
sometimes inclined to find the latter somewhat
stuffy and even old-fashioned. Pedro, with his
pipe, moustache, upper-class accent and slightly
detached air was the archetypal public-school
Englishman, but his leadership skills and care for
his men commanded respect from all ranks and
all nationalities.

On 2 April Pedro wrote to his distraught sister
who, with her baby daughter, had arrived at
Ootacamund:

'My Darling Rachel,

I have been waiting to write to you for a long time but could not until I got your new address. I can't tell you how very sorry and upset I feel for you, Rachel, you must have been going through absolute hell. I only hope we get good news of Hector soon.

'I am just praying I can take my squadron out against the Japs one of these days but unfortunately have my hands full with Huns and Its [Italians] *for the time being. Anyway I suppose whoever one is fighting it all comes to the same thing. Let's hope it will be all over soon, I've been sick of it for a long time.*

'If you take my advice, go home as there is nothing you can achieve by remaining where you are. Failing that, go to South Africa but please don't stay where you are. Another thing, don't dream of going to Colombo.

'I hope both you and Henrietta are fit — thanks for the photos. I am looking forward to seeing my goddaughter. I have started a savings bank for her which I expect she will blow like we all did with ours!

'I got command of the squadron recently so am now a squadron leader! Can you beat it! Promotion is pretty swift in the RAF but I think I have now reached my peak. I am very busy and have a really first-class squadron. The desert is a pretty

bleak place to live in; however it is the ideal place for a war as there are no buildings and no inhabitants to disturb or destroy.

'Do write to me and take my advice about going home.

With much love to both of you,

Tiggy.'

Rachel did not take his advice and remained in India for the duration of the war.

As squadron commander Pedro's first time in contact with the enemy was the next day when eight of his Kittyhawks in company with ten from elsewhere were detailed to accompany SAAF Bostons whose task was to bomb Derna on the coast north-west of Martuba. Over the Gulf of Bomba they were met by Messerschmitts and Macchi 202s (Italian fighters). Hindle claimed one Bf109 and a probable MC202 while Pedro and Flight Sergeant Carlisle jointly claimed a second German aircraft.

Early in the morning of 25 April twelve Ju87 bombers escorted by eight Bf109s and with a top cover of fifty-nine assorted German and Italian fighters, took off to attack allied shipping in Tobruk harbour. Eight Kittyhawks of 260 and twenty-three Tomahawks of 2 and 4 Squadrons of the SAAF were scrambled to intercept them. Six of Pedro's aircraft made the first contact, catching eleven Ju87s as they finished bombing. Pedro shot down one of the 87s and also claimed an MC202 destroyed and one more as a probable; he was then hit and had to force-land near Gazala from where he safely returned to the squadron at Gasr el Arid. Three other 260 pilots also claimed German victims.

For this action Pedro was awarded a Distinguished Flying Cross (DFC). The citation, published in May, read:

> *'In April 1942, this officer led a successful sortie against an enemy force of bombers, escorted by fighters, which attempted to raid Tobruk. At least four of the raiding aircraft were destroyed of which Squadron Leader Hanbury destroyed one. This officer continued to engage the enemy until his aircraft was so extensively damaged that he was compelled to land. Throughout he displayed magnificent leadership and courage. Squadron Leader Hanbury has destroyed at least five enemy aircraft.'*

Pedro wondered whether this would mean that he would have to go to "Buck House" after the war to collect his medal. If so, he decided, he would take the whole family to the palace and 'have a good feed on the house'!

During the last days of April HRH The Duke of Gloucester, the King's brother, arrived in North Africa to visit front-line squadrons. Flying in a Hudson, he was escorted safely into the airstrip at Gambut by Pedro and a number of his aircraft –

but not without incident. The Hudson's pilot overflew Gambut westwards, heading for enemy lines only thirty miles away at around 180 miles an hour. In order to turn him, Ron Cundy had to fly perilously close to the Hudson's wingtips until, not before time, the pilot got the message.

An unusual and welcome diversion for Pedro took place on 28 April when he flew as a passenger in a captured Junkers Ju52/3m – now the Luftwaffe's main transport aircraft but some of which had been in service with the civilian South African Airways before the war. Called The Libyan Clipper, it flew a round trip to Amriya and back to Gambut via the strip at Maaten Bagush, picking up goodies such as fresh food and, above all, beer. Other privileges also now came Pedro's way: as the squadron's senior officer he was entitled to a staff car, a Ford shooting-brake driven by Leading Aircraftsman Pete "Taxi" Sturgeon who had owned a London black-cab before the war.

As April turned into May, both sides in the Desert War began to envisage a new offensive to break the apparent deadlock. Axis aircraft in the theatre still outnumbered those of the allies, although the latter's serviceability rate was considerably higher. Hard as the ground crews worked to keep allied aircraft in the air, their efforts would need to redouble in the months to come.

Meanwhile, 260 Squadron continued its programme of offensive sweeps interspersed by flying top cover for the Bostons and the occasional emergency scramble. The squadron received an influx of seven Canadians, some like Eddie Edwards were experienced flyers, others were almost straight from training. They were soon in action: on 21 May nine Kittyhawks took off to carry out a sweep in the Tmimi-Gazala area, attacking two Bf109s, one of which Tom Hindle shot down. The next day on a similar mission Sergeant Carlisle claimed what Pedro described as 'a probable wop' (an MC202) and on the 23rd the squadron carried out a diversionary attack on Tmimi (the real target of the Bostons being Derna) during which Pedro severely damaged a Bf110 on the ground at Martuba.

As June approached, the squadron redeployed to Gambut only forty miles from the Egyptian border, and on the 27th the Afrika Korps began its major push east in an attempt to take Alexandria and then Cairo. The following day 260 Squadron was in the air for a total of four and a half hours as Air Vice-Marshal Coningham responded to the 8th Army's plea that air supremacy operations should be suspended to concentrate on ground-attack sorties against Axis columns on the move.

On the last day of the month, an Australian of 260, Flying Officer John Waddy shot down a Ju87 when on a bomber escort mission and also claimed two probables (later confirmed as kills but not recorded), but May nevertheless ended on a sour note as Tom Hindle, on his third sortie that day and, by all contemporary accounts exhausted, was killed. As a hugely experienced desert warrior and a steadying influence to the young he would be sadly missed – not least by his squadron leader. Ron Cundy recorded at the time that under normal circumstances Hindle could have handled the two Bf109s which shot him down in flames, but that tiredness must have caused him to make a fatal mistake.

June was a disastrous month for the allied ground forces. After a gallant defence by the Free French in the early stages of a general withdrawal, Bir Hacheim was lost and, as Rommel advanced, air force units too had to fall back. On 7 June 260 Squadron moved its base to Bir el Beheira closer to the Egyptian border. The Kittyhawk pilots were now almost continuously in the air; on the 8th Pedro flew four sorties, sweeping over Bir Hacheim and escorting the Bostons as they tried desperately to bomb the German columns.

The Boston squadrons themselves were worked even harder, their ground crews digging slit-trenches and sleeping next to their aircraft to cut down turn-round times. Dirty, dishevelled and weary in the extreme, British, Australian, Canadian, New Zealand and South African pilots flew relentlessly in support of the withdrawing 8th Army in an attempt to stem the German tide. But the Afrika Korps was not to be denied; Rommel, understanding that this would be his final attempt to take Egypt, pressed on.

Pushed off the Gazala Line on the 12th, the Allies lost Tobruk less than a week later and by the 24th had fallen back 350 miles to a line running south from the coastal village of El Alamein into the Qattarra depression, fewer than sixty miles west of Alexandria. Continuous sandstorms made flying difficult in the first few days of the month and there were storms, too, on the ground.

At 260 Squadron's base Pedro had called his pilots together to remind them in terms not open to argument that he would not tolerate 'line-shooting' – that is exaggerated claims as to air-craft shot down or damaged. So stern was he in this respect that Eddie Edwards recorded that most of the pilots would have volunteered for dangerous missions rather than make a claim to the commanding officer with only scanty details! Hanbury also sacked his intelligence officer – the officer responsible for briefing pilots and keeping records – so that until a replacement arrived in August record-keeping in the squadron was at best haphazard and sometimes inaccurate.

While leap-frogging eastwards (one half of the ground crews would stay with the aircraft until the other half was established at a new base) 260 Squadron flew fifty-six operational sorties that month engaged variously in bomber escort duties, dive-bombing, ground-strafing and inter-ception patrols with anything from four to twelve aircraft, depending on serviceability.

On the 15th the squadron had carried 500lb bombs slung on racks between the undercarriage, and having provided close cover to Bostons bombing panzer divisions south of Tobruk, they returned to the target area, diving down to 1,500 feet before pulling out and releasing their bombs on concentrations of enemy vehicles. This opera-tion was repeated twice that day and again on the

16th. From Bir el Beheira, through LGs 76 (south of Sidi Barrani), 115 (Sidi Haneish, south-east of Maaten Bagush) to 09 (ten miles west of Daba, which the ground crews left only when enemy tanks were within two miles), they reached LG97 at the end of June, one of a clutch of over a dozen landing grounds near Amiriya on the Alexandria-Cairo road.

On the 27th eight Kittyhawks led by Hanbury took off to escort nine Bostons in an attack on a German-occupied landing ground between Sidi Barrani and Mersah Matruh. They were inter-cepted by six Bf109s and in the ensuing mêlée Pedro claimed one Bf109 and another probable while Sergeant Parrott also claimed one Messerschmitt.

Although June had been calamitous for the ground forces, 260 Squadron – and indeed 233 Wing as a whole – had performed particularly well. During the first twenty-three days of the German offensive not one Allied bomber had been lost to Axis fighter aircraft. But the squadron had paid a heavy price: since Pedro took over command fourteen of his pilots had been shot down of which (by the end of June) only one had been confirmed as a prisoner of war. Had they not all been so tired, he wrote to his father 'I probably would not have lost so many'. In recognition of his part in this operational excellence Pedro was awarded a Bar to his DFC, the citation being pub-lished at the end of July:

'This officer continues to display outstand-

ing skill, courage and fine leadership. Under his leadership his squadron has inflicted heavy losses on the enemy both in air combat and on the ground.

'During a recent sortie he led a formation as escort to our bombers far behind enemy lines and heavy damage was caused. All our bombers returned safely.'

The sortie referred to was probably one flown by 260 on 12 June when they escorted bombers on a mission west of El Adem.

Sergeant Pilot Ron Cundy was a little hazy on the subject of the party which followed the announcement of Pedro's award which had reached them unofficially down the Desert Air Force grapevine on 16 July:

'For reasons unknown (!) I led the squadron the next morning as top cover escorting Bostons to bomb a target south-west of El Alamein. I doubt whether any of us were fit to fly much less perform operationally after the celebrations of last night. Fortunately the enemy chose to ignore us and the operation was completed without incident.'

As the situation stabilised with the Allied forces entrenched behind the El Alamein lines, Cairo was in chaos as a hysterical fear of invasion took hold. Demonstrators tore down British propaganda posters and press correspondents encouraged disruption by blaming inefficiency in the British High Command for the loss of Tobruk and the subsequent retreat. Plans were prepared for the evacuation of the Desert Air Force southwards, and 260 Squadron in company with the others was placed on twelve hours notice to move. But the Afrika Korps had run short of both ammunition and fuel. Subjected now to intensive allied bombing, they dug in. For the moment there was a stalemate.

Pedro's final flight with 260 Squadron in this phase of the war was also on 16 July when he took off once more on an escort mission. His trip lasted ten minutes before he had to land again with an engine-bearing failure. On this disappointing note his operational tour came to an end and he was posted to 211 Group Headquarters at El Amiriya both as a controller and to help convert fighter units to fighter-bombing. He had in his three and a half months commanding the squadron made a considerable mark, and during his time in the western desert had personally accounted for five and a half enemy aircraft destroyed with two further probables and one Messerschmitt badly damaged.

In a letter to his father he confessed that he could 'do with this rest as we have been pretty hard worked of late'. He also floated the idea that it 'would be an excellent idea to get some old pilots to manage houses [pubs] after the war as they would be a terrific draw to anyone with interests in the RAF of which there will be thousands everywhere'. He then had second thoughts, reflecting that temperance might possibly be a problem: 'Not that they are drunkards but they do drink a considerable amount in the hours of darkness – although it doesn't seem to do them any harm!'

Little more is known of his enforced four months on the ground except that during a fortnight's leave he re-visited Palestine and Syria. He had nurtured a hope that he might have been allowed to go home to marry Patricia as, with exquisite timing, a cable had arrived from her on the day of his aborted sortie saying 'Yes'. He immediately wrote an airgraph (airmail flimsy) to break the good news to his parents and asked them, when they next had Patricia to stay, to take her into Manchester to buy an engagement ring:

 'Do see that she gets a really nice one (limit £50). I can easily afford that and will let you have a cheque within the next couple of months. The reason I ask you to do that is that I have had no statement from my bank for some time and don't want to write out a cheque which might not be met. Please don't think that this is a method of asking you for money as I would not dream of letting any one else pay for the ring but think that Patricia should have one as soon as possible. Please see that it is a good one as she will probably try and choose something terrible

worth about a fiver!

Love to all,

Tiggy.'

The engagement was tremendous news for his friends in the desert as well as his family and Beresford who, as commander of 233 Wing had been personally responsible for ordering Pedro to rest, tried to help him get permission to fly home for a few days. Sadly this was not to be, but Barney was in no doubt as to the depths of Pedro's feelings. After the war, in a letter to Patricia, he wrote: 'We all knew he was in love with you. He never talked much about it but he did occasionally. Furthermore he was inspired by something and that something was you.' The engagement was publicly announced by both *The Times* and *The Irish Times* on 19 August 1942.

On 20 September he wrote to Rachel from group headquarters:

'My dearest Rachel,
Thank you for your cable. It was one of the first I got about my engagement so I was very pleased to have it from you.
'I am investigating the possibility of coming down to India on my next ten days leave to visit you. It might be possible with very careful planning, flying all the way, and if it is I should love to do it. If I do, it

106

would probably be in a couple of month's time.

'I am at the moment what is known in the Air Force as a stooge or staff officer! I hate it (as you know I always disliked military discipline) but hope to be out of it soon.

'I have been away from home about fifteen months now and it's hard to imagine things there. Philippa must be very nearly grown up — she certainly writes as if she was. I think it's fine the way the entire family are doing war work at home. You should have seen Dad in his Home Guard uniform, he really was terrific! I met a lot of his men one time when I was on leave and they all thought the world of him.

'I had a bit of leave the other day in Alexandria and Cairo which was a most welcome change after the hectic time we had in May and June.

'Well, much love to you and Henrietta,

Yours,

Tiggy.

P.S. Do drop a line to Patricia. I know she would appreciate it.'

Sadly the tentative plan to fly to India to see his sister did not prove possible.

Although it was difficult for people to write to Tiggy to congratulate him, the avalanche of mail reaching Patricia almost overwhelmed her. On 20 August she replied to letters from Betty and Doddy saying that she had always wanted a sister and now she was about to have four – even if they were only to be in-laws! She added:

> *'Please forgive a joint letter but I have such a pile to answer I hardly know where to begin. Thank you so much for your good wishes to us both; I am feeling so happy I can hardly believe what has happened to me and now that it has come out in the papers, I feel more thrilled than ever. I feel so proud of Tiggy, it is really wonderful what he has done.'*

Denied his home leave, Pedro spent the next few months lobbying incessantly to be back with 260 Squadron. But life at 211 Group had some – if minor – compensations, including an improvised fox hunt mounted on American jeeps and following three hounds. Despite the difficulties they managed after only half an hour to account for 'a fine red dog-fox'. Another attempt was made when Charles Coles came to stay at group head-quarters, but this time without hounds. The fox suffered the indignity of being fired at by revolvers from a jeep travelling across the desert at forty miles an hour before going safely to ground. At the beginning of November, a bored Pedro at last had his way and was flying opera-tionally over the western desert once again.

Chapter Six

THE DESERT WAR – PEDRO'S RETURN

The arrival of Lieutenant-General Bernard Montgomery to command the 8th Army led to a complete change of mental attitude among the allies in North Africa – not only the ground troops but also the air forces were re-galvanised. Montgomery arrived in Cairo on 12 August and within three days had ordered the destruction of all contingency plans dealing with further withdrawal. 'If we cannot stay here alive', he said in an address to senior officers, 'then let us stay here dead'. Unhappy with the geographical separation of his own headquarters and that of the Desert Air Force, he ordered their co-location at Burg-el-Arab, about halfway along the coast road between Alexandria and El Alamein.

Montgomery expected Rommel to try and resume his eastward march to the south of the El Alamein line and so strengthened his forces on the Alam-Halfa ridge. The Desert Air Force meanwhile was concentrating on the heavy bombing of the harbour at Tobruk to deny the Afrika Korps the reinforcements and combat supplies it needed. With Tobruk made almost useless to him by this destruction, Rommel was forced to use the port at Benghazi, so far west in Libya that by day it was out of range (except from Malta) of allied aircraft, although Wellington bombers from Egypt frequently attacked it by night. But this meant the Germans had to transfer supplies over long distances to Egypt by road and rail, giving both bombers and ground-attack aircraft additional targets, or by inshore barges – a favourite quarry of allied Beaufighter aircraft with their long range and ten forward-firing 20mm cannon and .303inch guns. The Desert Air Force was now at a strength of twenty-one squadrons – including three of Spitfires who were able to sweep high over the battle area and attack Bf109s from above.

Apart from the intensive bombing raids August was mainly quiet. The personnel of 260 Squadron under the command of Squadron Leader Paul Devenish, a Rhodesian, lived more comfortably than ever before in North Africa. Shops, restaurants – and other more basic amenities – were available in abundance in Alexandria, and the men's daily menus now regularly included fresh food and such luxuries as chicken, green vegetables and fruit. Ron Cundy, Australian to the core, was particularly delighted that he could now get mint sauce! And then, on 30 August, Rommel launched his long-awaited attack on Alam-Halfa. This petered out after only a few days but air activity during September was intense. Unlike Hanbury, who flew practically every squadron operation himself (particularly the most dangerous sorties), Devenish believed in delegation. This hardly mattered as more than a few of the more senior (in terms of service) pilots in 260 had by now acquired much desert experience. This priceless asset was to be found mainly among the surviving non-commissioned pilots: Sergeants Eddie Edwards and Ron Cundy both found themselves not only leading flights of 260, but often the whole squadron. Cundy even on occasion led the wing on patrols, something that the rank-conscious South Africans were not happy about. Later on when Ron had been commissioned, the protests faded away.

On the evening of 23 October more than 1,000 British and allied guns opened the biggest artillery barrage since the First World War on the narrow front between El Alamein and the Qattara Depression. Twenty minutes later infantry and armour began to roll west. On 4 November 260 Squadron welcomed back Pedro Hanbury for another tour in command; there were many new faces for him to assimilate: Ron Cundy was the only pilot who had been with him for the whole of his first tour.

Almost coinciding with Pedro's return was the arrival of a recently commissioned intelligence officer by the name of Christopher Lee, later to become a famous actor. Hanbury had not been impressed by the general run of officers assigned to this very important role. One he had sacked and others had come close to being posted. His greeting to Lee was to the point: 'Put one foot wrong, my son, and you're out,' he said. 'Right, now let's go and get pissed.' Lee was to remain with 260 until the end of the desert war and established a relationship of mutual respect with his boss – but any leg-pulling was strictly one way. At one de-brief, Hanbury reported that he'd knocked out a couple of trucks, some horse-drawn vehicles and 'put a couple of nuns out of commission'. Lee could not believe his ears and diffidently asked his squadron leader whether he had heard correctly. 'Of course', said Pedro testily. 'Pregnant nuns, of course', he added. The story soon got round and for some time afterwards, Lee was plagued by radio messages from fellow intelligence officers in other squadrons enquiring what 260's latest tally of pregnant nuns amounted to.

Once the Axis line was broken, the 8th Army's advance was swift. As the ground forces moved inexorably westwards into Libya, so the squadrons of the Desert Air Force attacked Axis airfields and the ground troops of the Afrika Corps with ever increasing ferocity. Pedro's squadron was now moving its base every four or five days. On 6 November they were at LG 75 to the south of Sidi Barrani and on the 11th, in company with two SAAF units, they took off from Sidi Azeiz, just inside Libya, carrying 500lb bombs to attack targets immediately south of Tobruk. Seeing fifty enemy aircraft on the ground at Gambut Pedro ordered a change of plan; the bombing was accurate and fires began. Immediately afterwards Pedro's section was jumped by two Bf109s. He was able to get in a burst at one with no observable results but his companions, Sergeants Williams and Hill turned away, leaving themselves vulnerable. Williams got his damaged aircraft safely back to Mersah Matruh but Hill was shot down and taken prisoner. Ron Cundy shot down a German Storch reconnaissance aircraft and other pilots of the squadron accounted for a Ju88.

The next move to Gazala, forty miles west of Tobruk, came only four days later and this was followed by another forty-mile jump to Martuba, inland from Derna – a sure indication that the German withdrawal was almost headlong. During the first evening in the mess at Martuba, Ron Cundy announced to his squadron leader that he had now completed 199 hours and forty minutes of operational flying. Pedro suggested that he should forego the last twenty minutes and stand down from operations. Cundy was tempted but felt sure he would regret it. 'Right, you stubborn bugger,' said Hanbury, 'I've got a good one for you tomorrow. We're strafing a Jerry landing ground at Magrun.' This was not at all what Ron wished to hear: not only was Magrun 200 miles away, active enemy airfields were notoriously well defended. He could not, however, back down but in the event the seven aircraft, led as always by Hanbury, never completed their mission, being thwarted by bad weather. Cundy landed safely back at base having flown a total operations tour of 202 hours and ten minutes.

The Australian was now officially posted to group headquarters but Pedro intervened. He had heard of a captured Heinkel 111 in good condition on the ground at Derna, having been abandoned by the retreating Luftwaffe. This could, once repainted in squadron colours, be a useful addition to 260. All sorts of goodies could be carried from Alexandria – even Cairo – with such an aircraft. He sent Ron to inspect it and he discovered that the Germans had also thoughtfully left behind a brand new engine, still crated, together with an instructional handbook. One of 260's ground staff understood technical German and the engine was soon changed; the Heinkel was now serviceable and named The Delta Lily. Next came the question of who was to fly it. Cundy had never flown an aircraft with more than one engine and neither had anyone else in the squadron. Hanbury, however, was cheerful: 'It'll be easy,' he said, 'it's just got two of everything instead of one.' He did not, however, volunteer to fly it himself. In the event Cundy tracked down an American, an extremely laconic Texan, who claimed some twin-engined experience – it later turned out to be a total of only five hours! After a couple of dual-control trips which were not without their hairy moments, Cundy felt that he had learned enough of the rudiments. It would be safer, he thought, if he perfected his techniques without the help of his instructor. By the end of the first week in December he was flying a regular milk run, not only to collect food and drink, but to take as many as nine pilots at a time for a night out in Alexandria. These trips were not always trouble free – despite its new markings the Heinkel, on more than one occasion, attracted anti-aircraft fire from allied gunners.

On 14 December, while on a dive-bombing mission to El Agheila, on the coast 120 miles south of Benghazi, Pedro and his squadron were jumped by eight Bf109s and were forced to jettison their bombs short of the target. Hanbury and Sergeant Bill Stewart managed bursts at two of the enemy, both claiming damage. Two Kittyhawks were also damaged, one getting home safely to Belandah, where 260 was now based, and the other crash-landing at Magrun. During the week before Christmas worse was to come as the squadron lost one of its veterans, Flight Sergeant Norman McKee who had arrived in May with Eddie Edwards. Another of that group, Sergeant Jack Takvor, was lost three days later when he had to bail out over the sea having been hit by flak. He was never seen again.

The squadron moved west once more on the 18th, this time to a strip near Marble Arch, the huge folly built by Mussolini of stone shipped from the Seven Hills of Rome. This hideous structure on the border between Cyrenaica and Tripolitania celebrated the Italian conquest of Libya and carried images of Mussolini and the King of Italy. It had been a favourite – but curiously undamaged – target of Allied bombers as they passed by on more important missions. For 260 and the other constantly moving squadrons, occupying a former German landing ground was fraught with hazard. Anti-tank and anti-personnel mines had inevitably been planted in and around both the strip and surrounding ground, so that engineers had first to undertake the considerable work involved in making the area safe. But the army was now in such a hurry that on this occasion personnel of 260 had to clear most of these explosives themselves, learning in the process that fiendish booby traps had been planted in the most unexpected places. Christopher Lee recorded that he would never again pick up an Iron Cross unless the wearer was still alive!

20 December proved to be arguably the worst day for 260 Squadron since its arrival in the Middle East. At 0725, twelve Kittyhawks led by Pedro, left Marble Arch on a strafing mission west of Tamet. They had just completed the operation and, therefore, were almost out of ammunition, when they were attacked from above by four Bf109s. Flight Lieutenant Vic Thagard RCAF, Flight Sergeant Red McClive (an American who had joined the RCAF early in the war) and Sergeant Dick Adams RAF were shot down in flames, Thagard and McClive being killed. Two more – Pilot Officer Jack Sheppard and Sergeant John Colley, both RAF – were badly shot up but managed to crash-land. One Messerschmitt only was damaged. Strange as it might appear, there was little evidence of grief among the pilots of 260

in the wake of these losses. The survivors had grown so accustomed to their friends being shot down that it was simply taken as a matter of course. Far more to the point was the private and personal conjecture going through everyone's mind as to who was going to be the next to die. To this question every pilot, had they been asked, would have answered 'Well, it won't be me'. Their only raison d'etre was the killing of Germans; the more that were destroyed the higher the chance of survival. Ron Cundy once remarked to Pedro that, despite, everything, he could not hate the enemy pilots. Hanbury looked at him, eyes blazing: 'You've got to hate them Ron,' he said. This was the last squadron contact with the enemy for ten days, and 260 turned its attention to Christmas.

The squadron Heinkel now came into its own and on 21 December Cundy and a few others were despatched by Pedro to Alexandria. As this letter from Marble Arch demonstrates, the squadron leader was determined that his men should eat and drink the finest fare that Ron could find:

'Dear Mum and Dad,
Have been so busy advancing lately that I've had no time for writing. These Huns are as fast as the Wops when they really start running. I expect we'll have a bit of a scrap down Agheila way but we still hope to spend Christmas in or near Tripoli. In fact we are planning terrific parties and are going to bring up

turkeys and all the Christmas fare in a captured German bomber I got hold of for the squadron. It is a Heinkel 111 (one of those that used to bomb Manchester) and my mechanics now have it in working order. I estimate that stripped of its war equipment it will carry 6,000 tins of beer or 100 turkeys! Anyway it's a grand acquisition and has been christened The Delta Lily and has a crest of a scarlet shield with a tin of frothing beer.

'I have had a lot of shooting during the last few days and two of us had a bag of thirty chicaw (a sort of partridge), ten golden plover and fifteen duck. All of these have proved marvellous eating after a diet of bully beef.

'Tomorrow I fly to the delta [Alexandria] for a couple of days leave and general wash up, haircut and, I am sorry to say, de-lousing. We are on an ex-Italian drome and the place is full of them. However as long as we advance who cares?

'Isn't the war news terrific? You should see the stuff the Hun has left behind and some of the miserable prisoners that go by every day – utterly demoralised. Nobody bothers to collect the Its, so they get into their own trucks and drive to Alexandria and give themselves up. I've actually seen them going along the road; no guards or anything.

'We had a thoroughly agreeable time

bombing and strafing retreating columns (chiefly German) all the way from El Alamein to Agedabia and caused considerable destruction for the loss of only two pilots from my squadron. The Luftwaffe has had such a towsing that we did not see much of him.

Love to all,

Tiggy.'

Cundy landed The Delta Lily at Mariyut, very close to Alexandria, and set off for the Agnides emporium run by the eponymous Greek trader who, even in wartime, could lay his hands on most of the world's finest produce. In three days all was assembled and the Heinkel's capacious bomb-bay was packed with turkeys, legs of pork, whisky, beer, fresh fruit, vegetables, nuts, raisins and all the other essentials of Christmas. Fifty cauliflowers could not be accommodated with the rest so they had to go in the fuselage with the passengers. So heavily laden was the aircraft that Cundy only just managed to get it off the ground as Lake Mariut loomed ever more quickly at the end of the runway. Towards the end of his four-hour trip, he heard on the radio some jumbled messages which seemed to indicate that several Ju88s had chosen that day to attack the allied forward landing grounds. They were chased off by Kittyhawks of 3 Squadron RAAF who then turned their attention to the Heinkel, frightening the wits out of Cundy who did not realise for some time that they were well aware of his identity and were only mobbing him up! Christmas was celebrated in great style – even 3 Squadron was sent a gift of beer – and at dinner the non-commissioned ranks were, as tradition demanded, waited upon by the officers. Pedro had by now learned to fly the Heinkel, as had a couple of others, but the luxury was short-lived. By the end of January 1943, 260 Squadron's prize possession had been confiscated by the Aircraft Intelligence Service for examination.

Despite his frantically busy days, Pedro remembered his family at Christmas, sending home a cheque for £15: 'Five for Henrietta's savings book, five for mine and five for useful presents for you [his mother], Dad and the bints. If I find a friend who is flying home I will send my Christmas presents with him. If not I'll keep them here until I come home.' He had now taken to referring to his unmarried sisters as the bints, a not altogether flattering Arabic word for girls!

The squadron was now converting to Mk III Kittyhawks and its last operational flight of 1942 on 30 December ended in triumph. Eight of the new aircraft, led by the newly commissioned Eddie Edwards, had taken off at 1220 for an interception patrol over Bir el Zidan. Finding themselves high above six Bf109s diving to strafe allied ground troops, Edwards ordered his men to attack, shooting down one and damaging another himself before his guns seized; the other two pilots in his section, Flying Officer Thornhill and

Pilot Officer Jack Sheppard each got one, and in the top-cover section Flying Officer Fallows RNZAF and Pilot Officer Doug England RAF both succeeded in downing one each. On returning to Marble Arch, Edwards's men filed their reports claiming five kills and one damaged – the latter being later reported as destroyed by an army observer. This was one of the most successful single engagements in the history of the squadron and Flight Lieutenant Edwards's personal tally had now risen to twelve and a half destroyed.

On the last day of the year the squadron moved to Gzina, a landing ground away from the coast, 25 miles south-east of Sirte where they became part of 3 SAAF (Fighter) Wing. There they celebrated New Year's Eve and said goodbye to Ron Cundy who, at his own request, was being posted home to Australia to defend his homeland against the Japanese: some townships in north and north-east Australia had been under bombing attack almost continuously in 1942. A number of senior officers tried to persuade him to stay but he was adamant. It wasn't until he arrived in Sydney that his father was able to tell him that he had been awarded a DFC, a DFM (Distinguished Flying Medal) and a Mention-in-Despatches. Pedro, who had been responsible for recommending him for all these awards, had not told him for fear of possible rejection of his reports, and confirmation had not come through until after Ron had sailed on the *Queen Mary*.

Hanbury had been disappointed that he had not flown with his men on 30 December but he was back in action on 2 January. News had reached the intelligence officer that a large number of Bf109s were on the ground at Churgia, south of Misurata. At 1025 eleven Kittyhawks led by Hanbury took off to strafe them. On their way to the target and only eight miles short, 260 flew over an enemy tank concentration. Here they came under heavy (but, luckily inaccurate) anti-aircraft fire, but the panzers were able to warn the Luftwaffe that Kittyhawks were heading in their direction. By the time Pedro and his men arrived at their target, five Bf109s had taken off and ten more were in the process of doing so. Hanbury attacked one which exploded in mid-air and Eddie Edwards fired at two more, one of which crashed. A fourth enemy aircraft was damaged by Flying Officer Perkins, an American who had joined the RAF. Two Kittyhawks came down: Flight Sergeant Mel Arklie RCAF, who had an engine failure, became a prisoner of war while Sergeant George Tuck RCAF crash-landed his badly damaged aircraft and although injured managed somehow to walk home to Allied lines. This engagement was the only one in which Eddie Edwards, who finished his war in May 1945 with a total of fifteen kills plus three shared, nine probables and thirteen damaged, was hit by enemy fighters; a remarkable statistic.

In the aftermath of Operation Torch, the successful American and British landings in Morocco and Algeria which put an end to Vichy French rule in those countries, Allied ground forces, including the 1st Army, had steadily advanced eastwards, the aim being to meet the 8th Army coming in the opposite direction and so squeeze the Axis powers out of North Africa. Progress had, however, been slow: the rain in January had made the mountain roads of Tunisia almost impassable and landing grounds had turned into treacherous bogs. In the air the Germans had been able to reinforce the Luftwaffe with fighter and fighter-bomber aircraft from Italy. The war was far from won.

260 Squadron began the year at Hamraiet, and settled into a steady routine of almost pure ground support which involved locating targets and going after them. In this role the Kittyhawks operated in sections of four aircraft which were permitted almost total independence. Making sure that enemy fighters were not around, the preferred method was to attack out of the sun, dive-bomb, strafe and then pull up quickly into the sun again to minimise the risk from anti-aircraft fire.

Operations were limited for the first few days both by sandstorms and then by determined attacks on the landing grounds at Hamraiet delivered by bomb-laden Bf109s. These were largely beaten off by Spitfires of 145 and 601 Squadrons but made for an uncomfortable time for those on the ground. On 12 January, 260 moved west again, this time to one of the many landing grounds at Bir Dufan, inland from Misurata. A week later they were at Sedadah and by the 24th, in company with the whole of the wing (now commanded by Wing Commander H.F. [Billy] Burton DFC and Bar) had reached Castel Benito, the main airfield serving the port of Tripoli which was in the hands

of the 8th Army, the Afrika Korps having with-
drawn to Tunisia. In a letter dated 2 February,
Pedro wrote home at length to describe his recent
adventures:

'We have had a great time during
the last few months. We would get
to one place, stay there for a few
days and then move on to the next. From
Agheila onwards it was all virgin country
to us and though there was plenty of desert
there were lots of things of interest. We
were in the advanced striking force the
whole time and so for about four or five
days out of every seven we would be doing a
lot of operations, chiefly bombing and
strafing Rommel's retreating motor transport and occasionally tickling up his air-
force on their landing grounds if they
started to get uppish. They did at the end,
as I think they had been cursed by Goering
and told to do or die. However I think they
were pretty well licked by the time we got to
Tripoli in spite of the fact that they had
their latest brand-new fighters straight out
from Europe. On the other two days of the
week we would probably be out of range and
have to move again. We have built our own
aerodromes as most of his (Rommel's) are
heavily mined and I lost a few trucks on
one of them.
'After Marble Arch you come to a series
of old fishing ports and running south

from these are huge wadis [river beds] *and ravines with quite a lot of vegetation. There we had quite a lot of gazelle and bustard which made an excellent change from bully beef and biscuits. After that we came to the hilly country and the beginning of growing crops, trees and green fields which was the scene of the last stand of the German forces before giving up Tripoli. It is a marvellous country from there on and I must say the Italians farmed it very well indeed. They tried to destroy their last big aerodrome near Tripoli* [Castel Benito] *by ploughing it up. We went and shot up their ploughs and they never finished the job. It is proving a very useful aerodrome for us.*

'Just before we took Tripoli, we decided that we should be the first Western Desert Air Force squadron to fly over Tunisia. So four of us took off about four hours before dawn in the waning moonlight. We passed over Tripoli which was well alight (the Huns were blowing up as much as they could) and went about 100 miles into Tunisia, crossing the coast north of Gabes. There we saw a lorry going along the road with its headlights on. Our first stick of bombs put the lights out.

'The next thing we knew we were slap over a Hun aerodrome and looking down we could see Heinkels and Ju88s all over the place. We were just turning round to strafe it when the Huns realised we were

hostile and every type of tracer bullet imaginable came after us, more alarming than really dangerous. Discretion being the better part of valour we continued on our way and found a small camp with troops around an early morning fire. They got a better warming up than they bargained for!

'It was still pretty dark and again we found ourselves over a Hun drome. This time we managed to get in a good strafe before the ack-ack could open fire and we destroyed a Heinkel on the ground. Then up came the ack-ack again, all colours of the rainbow, but no harm to us. The dawn came and we made our way home across the lower plains of Tunisia and Tripolitania, passing over an Arab village, a herd of gazelle and flocks of bustard. It was a most amusing morning.

'When Tripoli fell we moved into the green belt [Castel Benito] *and I managed to take over five blocks which were designed for Italian married officers. They are clean with baths, electric light and gardens – in fact everything. So for the first time in almost two years the whole squadron is living under roof. We have planted the garden with vegetables and I have bought a flock of thirty lambs so that we can have fresh meat twice a week once we move forward again. I now have a Messerschmitt fighter to replace The Delta Lily and also a couple*

of Fiat cars. There is a winery near by and, needless to say, I have enough chianti to last the mess for six months.

'Tripoli itself is very battered and very quiet. Most of the Italians have gone. I think it will improve in time. I am just going down to Cairo for a ten day course. I don't think it will be long before I come home. It may be with the fall of Tunisia, or sooner.

Love to all,

Tiggy.'

The four-Kittyhawk sortie described in the letter took place on 22 January and the second 'Hun drome' they found was Medanine, an airfield on the mainland south of Djerba Island. The Heinkel on the ground was destroyed by Flight Sergeant Thomas.

While Hanbury was away on his course there was news of some well earned decorations for pilots of 260 Squadron. Eddie Edwards was awarded a long-overdue DFM and a DFC. Newly promoted Flying Officer Bill Stewart, another Canadian, was also given a DFM while Pilot Officer Jack Sheppard RAF received the DFC.

During February the squadron had left the comforts of Castel Benito and moved, first to Sorman on the coast west of Tripoli, and then to El Assa, only five miles from the Tunisian border. Meanwhile the ground forces had closed in on the

Castel Benito airfield, January 1943. Pedro, in command of 260 Squadron is in front clutching what appears to be that evening's supper. In the doorway of his caravan are (inside) Corporal Lowry and, leaning against the doorway, Flight Lieutenant Eddie Edwards. The other pilots, left to right, are Flight Sergeant Bill Parlee, Sergeant Williams, Usher, Harvey, Flight Lieutenant Jeff Fallows, Flying Officer Thornhill and Nicholls.

heavily defended Mareth Line where Montgomery paused to receive reinforcements of both men and equipment. In preparation for the ground attacks to come the Desert Air Force began to attack Axis airfields with fighter-bombers while American and British squadrons from Algeria concentrated on targets in the area of the Kasserine Pass, about ninety miles west-north-west of Sfax.

260 Squadron was in the thick of these operations, and those that followed on enemy supply routes and the Mareth Line itself. The ground assault began on the night of 20 March 1943 and 260, now based at Medanine as a part of 239 (Offensive Fighter) Wing, took on a new role – that of seeking out and destroying individual tanks and guns actually engaged in the battle. On the morning of 26 March Hanbury briefed his men that later that day, the 8th Army was to create and break through a gap in the Mareth Line. Spitfires would fly continuous top cover and light bombers would drop their loads in the forward battle area. The Kittyhawks, in waves of thirty-six aircraft, would then dive-bomb targets marked by coloured smoke. Once the bombs had gone they would strafe targets behind the line.

The morning weather was not good: wind and dust-storms raged and the pilots watched the sky hoping for a break. At 1230 the skies cleared and at 1530, in company with two United States Army Air Force (USAAF) squadrons, 260's part in the operation began. Pedro raised his right arm above the cockpit and waved it in a circular motion. As one, his pilots pressed their starter buttons. The twelve Kittyhawks rolled forward, gathered speed and were airborne. Turning into position in front of the American squadrons they arranged themselves into three sections, Hanbury's leading. It was nearly 1600 hours when they reached 10,000 feet and saw the battle beneath.

Six minutes later they were there. Hanbury

gave the order 'switches on' to arm the two 250lb bombs each carried. At a sixty-degree angle the squadron leader's section started its dive; the pilots could now see the flashes from the lethal .88mm German anti-aircraft guns and the coloured smoke marking out their targets. By the time he had reached 3,000 feet, Pedro's speed was touching 450 miles an hour, and over the targets the pilots released their bombs and turned away to port, continuing down as they monitored the other aircraft carry out their missions. They watched in horror as two American aircraft went down in flames and no parachutes appeared. Now flying at only 300 feet above the valley floor and below the hilltops, 260 Squadron saw enemy tanks moving forward. Still in sections of four they turned to attack. Some enemy guns continued to fire and these Hanbury's Kittyhawks silenced at a range of 300 yards before flying further up the valley to strafe vehicles, guns and tents. Another run followed, shooting at everything in sight until, empty of ammunition, they headed for the nearest allied landing ground to refuel.

Two of Pedro's aircraft had been damaged and flew straight to Medanine and another landed with a hole in its tail-plane. Flight Lieutenant Jeff Fallows, the New Zealander, had forced-landed after the truck he had strafed blew up under him. He was taken prisoner. The American squadrons had been hit hard, four pilots had not returned and three others had crash-landed. Hanbury's remaining Kittyhawks refuelled and rearmed before taking off again at 1735. They would complete another run before returning home to Medanine and a welcome mug or two from the dozen bottles of champagne liberated from Djerba Island.

On 3 April 239 Wing moved to the landing ground at El Hamma, only recently vacated by the Luftwaffe. It became almost immediately apparent that this was too close to enemy lines for comfort. One flight of 260 had just landed when enemy Focke-Wulf (FW)190 fighter-bombers appeared overhead and dropped their lethal loads.

The first attack did little damage but they returned the next day to greater effect. El Hamma also came under fire from German artillery located in the hills some twelve miles away. Shells hit the wing headquarters tent, one Kittyhawk was destroyed and four Australian ground staff of 450 Squadron were killed. Wing headquarters, 112 and 450 Squadrons had had enough and moved back to Medanine. Hanbury, however, refused to move and 260, which was deployed on the south side of the landing ground, furthest from the shelling, stayed put.

At around this time, Pedro was surprised to get a message from a Royal Navy Motor Torpedo Boat base in Algeria that Charles Coles had gone missing on a mine-laying expedition. Coles claimed, in an article written after the war, that Hanbury led some of 260 Squadron on a search for him. This may well have been the case but in any event nothing came of it: Coles had been picked up by a German vessel and became a prisoner of war. As the conclusion of the war in North Africa approached, Pedro began to make some tentative plans for his forthcoming leave and what might happen afterwards. He shared them with Philip and Dodo:

> *'Whether or not I shall have to come back here I don't know yet. Unfortunately I have become a sort of specialist by now and I suppose I am more useful with this force than I would be with any other.*
>
> *'But still whatever happens I suppose one cannot grumble. Will you please have my best uniform pressed and squadron leaders stripes put on the arms and also have the* [DFC] *ribbon sewn on if you can find a military tailor locally. I will wire you as soon as I know for certain that I am coming and when I get there I will take the first possible train from London to Manchester. I will also arrange for Patricia to come down.'*

On 7 April the armoured cars of the 12th Lancers reconnaissance regiment from the 8th Army met a patrol from the United States II Corps driving east: the junction between the two allied armies was made. As Montgomery's troops advanced steadily up the Tunisian coast to Sfax, about halfway to Tunis from the Libyan border, 260 Squadron was flying two or three sorties a day, usually as top cover for other units involved in dive-bombing the enemy's supply routes. The Axis forces were now faced by a single united front closing in and driving them into an enclave around Tunis itself.

The allied air forces then embarked on Operation Flax, offensive action designed to cut the enemy's air routes between North Africa and Italy. On 17 April, 260 made its first interception sweeps over the Cap Bon peninsula. At just after 0800 Pedro led twelve Kittyhawks equipped with long-range tanks, over the cape and the sea beyond looking for enemy transport aircraft. Flying lower than usual he spotted four twin-engined Bf110s flying about 1,000 feet above them. 260 turned south, climbed and attacked. All the Messerschmitts were shot down: Flight Lieutenant Bill Stewart, Flight Sergeant Bill Parlee and Sergeant Rick Rattle, all Canadians, got one each and the fourth belonged to Hanbury who pursued his victim for thirty miles before bringing it down into the sea; it was to be his final kill.

The next day, now known as that of the Palm Sunday Massacre, saw fifty-nine Luftwaffe transports and sixteen escorting fighters, claimed by American pilots. During Operation Flax, more than 400 German transport aircraft had been brought down by allied pilots for the loss of only thirty-five fighters. It fell to Eddie Edwards to destroy the last of the transports, and with it the last confirmed victory of 260 Squadron in North Africa.

On 18 April the squadron moved for the final time in the campaign, occupying the airfield at Kairouan, Tunisia's most holy Islamic city, some seventy miles south of Tunis. It was there, a few days later, that Pedro received the unofficial news (it was not promulgated until the end of the month) that he had been awarded the Distinguished Service Order (DSO). This decoration, rarely given to a junior officer, is invariably the mark of outstanding leadership over a period of time: The citation read:

> *'This officer is an inspiring leader whose courageous example has contributed materially to the high standard of operational efficiency of the squadron he commands. In operations covering the great advance from El Alamein, Squadron Leader Hanbury led formations of aircraft with great skill, attacking and harassing the enemy with destructive effect. In attacks on the enemy's dispositions near Ksar Rhilane and at El Hamma, Squadron Leader Hanbury exhibited great dash. His fearlessness, efficiency and unswerving devotion to duty have been worthy of the highest praise.'*

Unofficial or not, the squadron knew how to celebrate such an event – as Pedro mentioned in a subsequent letter home on 24 April:

> *'Mail has become very spasmodic again. Have only had a couple of letters during the last fortnight, one from you and one from the bank! The pig* [liberated by 260 Squadron

ground crews from an Italian farm!] *is fat-tening up well so we are looking forward to the fall of Tunis. Had a celebration the other night (for the gong), from which I have not yet fully recovered!*

'I don't know whether Patricia would like to get married during this leave of mine. I am leaving it to her to decide. I'm afraid she will be very disappointed that it is not now definite that I am coming home for good. I'm afraid there is nothing more I can do about it for the moment as the offi-cial time out here is four and a half years for unmarried men (three and a half mar-ried), and I have only been out here for two years, coupled with the fact that they may want me specially for some job or other. I have no basic grounds for demanding a home posting in war time. However I think there may still be a 50 per cent chance; there is nothing I want more.

'If I do and get married will Patricia have to do war work? Have to put her in the WAAFs! [Women's Auxiliary Air Force]. *All is well with us here. We are in quite a pleasant place with farm land all round.*

Love to all.

Tiggy.'

He also wrote to Rachel on that day to tell her that all his efforts to go to see her in India had failed

The pig, liberated from an Italian farm, with which
260 Squadron was proposing to celebrate the fall of
Tunis which came on 13 May 1943.

and that he was going to spend his leave in
England. Curiously there is no mention of marriage in this letter which rather indicated that all
planning in that department – save naming the
actual day which would be dependent on his
arrival in England – had been taken out of his
hands by his mother, his bride-to-be and his
future mother-in-law. The mention of leave in his
letter home was the result of a promise made to
him and the other squadron commanders by
Wing Commander Burton that he would see to it
that they all went home for a few days as soon as
the Tunisian campaign ended. Meanwhile the
allied air forces continued to patrol the Gulf of

Tunis and further afield in overwhelming numbers to prevent both axis reinforcement and attempts to evacuate German and Italian troops and equipment to Italy. On the ground the 1st and 8th Armies tightened their scissors grip on Tunis and on 13 May the enemy surrendered. In his logbook Eddie Edwards wrote: 'War over in North Africa Desert. FINITO!'

By this time Hanbury had heard from Patricia that she definitely wanted to get married on his leave. He was relieved, believing that it would be silly to go on being engaged for years as they were both so sure of themselves. He was, however, worried that a wedding during what was likely to be a short leave would mean that he would be able to spend only a short time with his parents before (as he put it) 'I go honeymooning'. As he wrote home to share this concern someone came into the mess to tell him that Tunis had fallen and that operational flying in the desert had come to an end. This momentous occasion was celebrated by the pilots of 260 Squadron in a manner almost as dangerous as any of the sorties they had flown over the last two years. They were not alone: Christopher Lee, still the intelligence officer, wrote of South African pilots jacking up the tails of their Spitfires and blazing away in the general directions of mountains while a squadron leader, noted hitherto for impeccable sobriety, picked up a machine gun and shot the central pole away from the officers mess tent of another squadron – only to have his fire returned with interest. Most clearly of all, Lee remembered being Pedro's driver as 260 staged a tank battle of their own with the squadron's three-ton lorries standing in for the real thing. Like medieval jousters the lorries charged to and fro, while from the passenger seats, pilots took pistol pot-shots at their dearest friends as they narrowly passed each other by. It occurred to Lee that they had all come a long way to be done-in by a comrade in a lethal game of 'chicken'. But the angels who look after children and drunken pilots were alert to all the dangers. No one was hurt.

A week after the end of military action, 260 Squadron flew to Zuara on the Libyan coast between Tripoli and the Tunisian border. Here they rested to await transfer to Sicily and the resumption of their war. During his active service in the last two and a half years Pedro had become an ace. This term, invented by the French in the First World War, has never been formally recognised by the British authorities but is widely accepted to mean a pilot with five or more aerial victories to his credit. In May 1943 Hanbury's official tally in aerial combat read: 'Ten and two shared, destroyed; two probables; three and two shared, damaged.' He had thus been credited, entirely or partly, with the destruction, probable destruction or damage in the air of nineteen enemy aircraft – seventeen of them German and two Italian. This record takes no account of those many aircraft and other enemy machines of war destroyed on the ground or at sea.

260 Squadron was proud of its leader and was determined to give him a memorable stag night

on the eve of his departure for England and Patricia. During the revelry, Pedro's flying helmet was filled more than once with beer and then rammed down on its owner's head, becoming far too sodden for it to accompany him on leave. The pilots handed it for safe-keeping to "Taxi" Sturgeon who carefully washed and then stowed it in the bottom of his kit-bag hoping, as he put it after the war, 'to curry favour with the command-ing officer at a later date'. Nearly fifty years passed during which the helmet, still in Taxi's safe custody, fulfilled a number of roles ranging from use as a receptacle for street donations, to RAF charities, to many appearances on stage in Old Tyme Music Hall variety shows (Pete's post-war career), before he inserted an advertisement in *Air Mail*, the journal of the RAF Association, asking for news of Pedro's family to whom he would like to present the trophy. By an extraordi-nary set of coincidences, the advert produced the desired result and Hanbury's helmet came home.

Chapter Seven

HAPPINESS AND TRAGEDY

Although she had finally decided to become Mrs Osgood Hanbury in July 1942, Patricia's life changed little during the remainder of that year. For one thing she had no idea when she might see Tiggy again, or for how long, or in her darkest moments, whether she would ever see him at all. So life in Scotland went on with very few variations: Home Guard duties, social rounds, tennis parties in the summer and shooting in the winter all kept her busy.

In September she went down to London for a few days where she met Philip and Dodo Hanbury who, she recorded in a brief diary note, gave her the warmest of welcomes. The main purpose of this trip seems to have been the changing of her engagement ring which had proved not to be a good fit (although the new one was exactly as she had hoped), and to have her photographs taken for the pages of glossy social magazines in the wake of her engagement. She managed also to fit in a great deal of shopping, several visits to the cinema with girlfriends and more than a few drinks parties. By the end of the month she was back in Scotland and embarking with the Speed family on a trip to Islay where she stalked – killing her first stag – shot grouse and went hawking for both grouse and pheasants. In October Philip came to stay at Gortinane for just under a week during which Patricia was able to arrange for him three days shooting, two lunches and a church parade.

At the beginning of December she went home to Crossdrum for a month, travelling by train and steamer via Stranraer and Larne in Northern Ireland on the outward journey, and back from Dublin to Holyhead so that she could visit the Hanburys in Altrincham on her way to Scotland. The whole trip, including sleeping berths, was by no means cheap, costing £6 – more than £250 in today's money.

The announcement of the engagement had brought forth a steady stream of wedding present cheques, including £30 from her father and £25 from someone she noted as 'a friend' (considerable sums at that time) but, still not knowing when Tiggy would be coming home and whether, if he did, there would be time to get married, she made few arrangements for the first three months of 1943. It had, of course, fallen to the Harman parents to make such arrangements as they could during all this uncertainty.

One decision they were able to take was that the wedding should happen in England – Ireland was too far away from most of Patricia's and Tiggy's friends, and there was also the tricky question of Irish neutrality to consider. They contacted an old (and very rich) friend, Cyril Pekitt, a retired major of the Royal Sussex Regiment, and his wife Christine, who owned an exquisite moated former rectory in Chailey, a village seven miles from Lewes in East Sussex. The Pekitts had been at Chailey Moat only since 1938 but had known the Harmans well in the regiment. They responded in generous style, asking the Harman family to stay, offering their house for the wedding reception and persuading the rector of the parish church to standby to hold a wedding at short notice.

At the beginning of April Patricia knew from news of the desert war that Tiggy's leave would shortly be due, and having made her decision to marry she began to make her arrangements. During the first week of the month she was in London, buying first her wedding dress at Liberty's (white watered silk with a veil of Brussels lace) and then a 'going-away' outfit from Harrods. For this she was, as tradition demanded, funded by her father. Her own wedding present fund, now amounting to nearly £100, remained untouched: she wanted to consult Tiggy before spending any of it.

The month passed and then, with the minimum of warning Tiggy landed in the midst of his family. On 15 May a telegram reached Patricia at Gortinane; it was brief and to the point: 'Arrive Altrincham 18th early. Send your plans there. Leave arrangements to you. Love, Hanbury.' In the event he arrived in Cheshire on Wednesday the 19th, Patricia having hot-footed it down from Scotland two days earlier. They were all amazed at the physical and mental well-being of the man of the moment. Betty, who arrived with Doddy on the Thursday described him as 'sweet and happy and full of beans. He was thin but looking marvellously well and brown and telling amusing stories about the desert.'

The next day was spent on the telephone – to the Harmans, the Pekitts, the rector, and a host of others. On Friday the Hanbury family left home for the Dorchester Hotel in London where, missing only Rachel, they celebrated Tiggy's safe return and spent the night. Patricia, however, left them in London and travelled on to join her parents at Chailey. Somehow all was arranged and the next morning, Saturday 22 May, the Hanburys went down to Sussex and had lunch at Haywards Heath before going on to Chailey Church for the wedding at 2.30pm.

Considering the short notice there was a gratifyingly large turn-out of friends and family – joined by a sprinkling of villagers wanting to wish the couple well. Patricia had managed to scoop up one bridesmaid, aged about twelve and dressed in blue, and after Tiggy had tried to contact two or three special friends without success,

William Harman was drafted in to act as best man. Douglas Speed, who could not be there, wrote to Patricia from Gortinane to say that he had offered up a prayer for her and Tiggy at the time of the marriage service.

The honeymoon was largely spent in London at the Dorchester, from where, on 29 May, Tiggy found time to write to his mother who had not been well for some time:

> *'My dear Mum,*
> *Just a line to say how much we enjoyed our day with you on Friday* [21 May]. *I only wish it could have been longer. However, all in all I am very glad I got married on this leave as we will be able to settle down all the sooner when I finally get home.*
>
> *'I hope you recover completely soon and please don't overdo it; no housework or anything strenuous. I only hope the wedding was not too much for you. It was good to see you all again and I'll be back soon so don't worry.*
>
> *Love to all,*
>
> *Tiggy.'*

On Monday 31 May, the newly-weds went their separate ways, Patricia back to Chailey to join her parents who were still with the Pekitts, and Tiggy in military transport to the RAF station at

Portreath in Cornwall. Initially built early in the war as a fighter command station, Portreath was now the staging post for flights to and from the Middle East. Happily Tiggy's vehicle broke down and he made his way to Chailey for a brief but wonderful forty-eight hours spent on long walks and in making plans until, in the early morning of Wednesday 2 June, he set off again for Cornwall.

Immediately after her husband left, Patricia wrote to her mother-in-law saying how wonderful the ten days had been, and that Tiggy had told her he might well be back in three months. She added that she really must get on and train their new Labrador puppy ready for shooting when he returned, and also told Dodo (whom she called "Mops") that, when they got back to Crossdrum her parents would find her an Irish cook-general to help in the house in Altrincham.

The weather at Portreath was unseasonably foggy so that Wednesday night passed with no prospect of flying. On Thursday morning in clearing skies FK386, a Hudson aircraft of 117 (Transport) Squadron RAF, based in North Africa, was made ready for take-off to Gibraltar. At 0700 the crew: the pilot, Flying Officer J.B. Buckley, Flying Officer E. J. McSherney the navigator, and radio-operator, Flight Sergeant D. V. Edwards, were ready to go as they awaited their passengers. There were seven in all, led by Group Captain Robert Yaxley DSO MC DFC, a thirty-one-year-old Beaufighter pilot, the others being Wing Commanders Billy Burton, E. Paul, P. T. Cotton and J. Goodhead, and Squadron Leaders J.

K. Young and O. V. Hanbury. It is likely that of all this distinguished company Pedro was the unhappiest: he had had to leave his bride of only ten days and he absolutely hated being flown by anybody; in the air Pedro was well-known for liking to be in charge.

At 0737 hours the Hudson took off and headed for Gibraltar. Why it had been decided to fly in daylight instead of waiting for nightfall which was the usual practice of such transit flights, will never now be known for certain. The dangers of undertaking such a journey by day, however, were well understood: the Bay of Biscay, across which the flight-path would take them, was notoriously a favourite hunting ground of Luftwaffe fighter aircraft based in France; indeed only a few days earlier a civilian DC3 airliner en route from Lisbon to Bristol, carrying seventeen passengers including the actor Leslie Howard, had been shot down over the bay.

Also in the air on the morning of 3 June was Leutnant Heinz Olbrecht from the German unit 14 Staffel/Kampfgeschwader 40 flying a Junkers Ju88C-6, a long-range heavy fighter variant of the bomber. At 1018 hours, Olbrecht spotted the unarmed Hudson flying south at about 7,000 feet. He attacked it ten times, hitting the fuselage and wing. The left engine and wing caught fire and it fell into the sea from about 1,500 feet and exploded. Later that day the Hudson and its occupants were posted officially as 'missing'.

So soon after the wedding did this tragedy occur that the authorities had not yet been informed that Tiggy and Patricia had married and that she had become his next-of-kin. Accordingly, the telegram dreaded by every family and the subsequent official letter from the Casualty Branch of the War Office were sent to Philip at Altrincham:

'Sir,
I am commanded by the Air Council to confirm the telegram in which you were notified that your son, Acting Squadron Leader Osgood Villiers Hanbury DSO DFC and Bar, Royal Air Force, is missing as the result of air operations on 3rd June 1943.

'Your son was a passenger in a Hudson aircraft which set out from a base in the United Kingdom and failed to arrive at Gibraltar.

'This does not necessarily mean that he is killed or wounded, and if he is a prisoner of war he should be able to communicate with you in due course. Meanwhile enquiries are being made through the International Red Cross Committee, and as soon as any definite news is received you will at once be informed.

'If any information regarding your son is received by you from any source you are requested to be kind enough to communicate it immediately to the Air Ministry.

'The Air Council desires me to express their sympathy with you in your present

anxiety.
  '*I am, Sir, Your Obedient Servant,*

  J.A.Smith.'

Meanwhile the distraught Patricia remained at Chailey. Amidst her misery she roused herself to write to Dodo:

  '*My dearest Mops,*
  I have been trying to write to tell you how sorry I am for you all. I have been thinking of you so much. If only Tiggy is safe somewhere – and he must be. I feel so bewildered. I never thought this would happen to us. Everyone is being so kind but I don't know if I can bear all this awful waiting. It seems so long. It's all so simply ghastly; I can't think why it should happen to us when we were so happy together.
  '*I go to Scotland on Thursday 17th* [June] *so please let me know any news.*
  '*With love to you all and keep hoping and praying.*

  Patricia.'

Patricia was almost swamped with sympathetic letters from family, friends and RAF colleagues of Pedro's from North Africa and elsewhere. One came from Major Eric Saville SAAF who had taken over command of 260 Squadron, and who himself was to be killed within three months while on operations over Italy:

'Dear Mrs Hanbury,
I would like to express to you, both for myself and for the whole squadron, our deepest sympathy in your recent tragic loss. I have quite recently taken over the squadron from your husband, but in that short time have come to learn clearly just how much he was liked and respected by all who served under him.

'Personally I knew him over quite a considerable period – ever since one evening in October 1941 when his squadron landed on our aerodrome and we had the pleasure of entertaining the pilots. It was not until April 1942 when he took over command of this squadron that I came to know him as the completely fearless and always aggressive leader that he was. There is no need for me to enlarge on his achievements – his reputation speaks more for him than any words I can say.

'His squadron will always remember him as their beloved leader, who quailed at nothing, who was completely oblivious to personal danger or personal advancement, and who was always the first to recognise the achievements of others. He set a very high standard which will be extremely difficult to live up to.

'If I can be of any assistance to you; if

at any time you require any information or photographs, I will be only too pleased to help.

'I hope that time will heal the wounds that fate has inflicted upon you, and that the knowledge that your husband was a great and fearless man, will help to assuage the bitterness of your grief.

Yours sincerely,

Eric Saville.'

Perhaps the most meaningful support for a grieving bride came in August from the wife of Wing Commander Billy Burton:

'Dear Mrs Hanbury,
You will probably wonder who I am and why I am writing. You may remember meeting my husband, Wing Commander Burton at the theatre when we were both seeing Arsenic and Old Lace – I was just the other side of the gangway, and I wish now that I had come across and met you as I have so often thought about you since this terrible affair.

'I expect it came as an awful shock to you – it did to me. I never dreamt they would send them by day like that – I just never thought about anything going wrong on the journey back, though I was worry-

ing about the operational flying they would do when they got back.

'I wonder what your feelings are about it? I feel terribly strongly that my husband is alive, but of course it might just be wishful thinking. I cannot believe that eleven of them [in fact ten] could just have disappeared without leaving a trace, and no wireless message or anything.

'It was the most wicked thing to have sent them off by day. I had a letter from Air Vice-Marshal Broadhurst and he said that if he had been there he would never have allowed it, so someone is to blame.

'The thing I feel so bitter about is that both your husband and mine (and most of the others too) were crack pilots but they never even had a chance to defend themselves. Also if only they had gone on the Monday as arranged, the weather was lovely and they would have gone by night.

'I see you are a long way from London, I am near Epsom, about 18 miles south of town. But if you ever do come to London, perhaps you would come to meet me.

'One of the objects of writing is that I felt that if we next-of-kin were in touch with each other, then if any of us heard anything, either good or bad, we could let the others know. I met a pilot the other day who escaped through Spain and he told me that if they had all been picked up and landed in Spain, it might be months before *we hear as the Spanish authorities are very slack about giving the names to the British Attaché in Madrid. Of course everything hinges on how they were shot down and if they had time to get into their dinghies. It is just a nightmare isn't it and I can't believe it really happened, especially when we were all so very happy for that fortnight.*

'I hope you won't mind my writing like this, but as I say I have thought of you so much and you know how well I can understand your anxiety when I have the same myself. I pray we shall have good news soon.

Yours sincerely,

Jean Burton.'

During the first week in July Patricia Hanbury was not feeling at all well and went to see her doctor in Tayinloan. He told her she was probably pregnant and she hastened to share the news with Philip and Dodo asking them not to tell anyone until she was sure. But she also confided in Betty:

'Dear Betty,
I have been pretty rotten for the last ten days and keep having to retire to bed being very sick. Well, the doctor says it may be a baby, but not sure yet — just think a little Tiggy, you simply

must love it. If only I could let Tiggy know he would be so thrilled as he said he wanted quite a lot! Oh dear me.

'I told your mother and she is pleased so I do hope you will be. I don't want anyone outside the family to know yet just in case it isn't that after all. I find myself lying in bed thinking of all the girl's and boy's names I like best.

Love

Patricia.'

Meanwhile Patricia, Jean Burton and the other widows lived in the desperate hope that their husbands might somehow be still alive until, a year later, in July 1944, the Air Ministry officially presumed that all those in the Hudson had lost their lives. During that time, only one shaft of light had illuminated Patricia's dreadful darkness, the birth of Christopher Osgood Philip Hanbury at Crossdrum on 16 February 1944. Among his godparents were Barney Beresford and Charles Coles, although the latter was still in his German prison camp from which he was not released until May 1945. Beresford, now stationed in England, hastened to accept Patricia's invitation, adding:

 'Without Pedro it would have been impossible for his squadron to have attained those amazing

heights when the battle was going at its worst. He is courage personified and an inspiring example to all of us who worked with him.

'May God bring him safely home and in the meantime may his son grow up in the sure knowledge that his father is one of England's greatest heroes.'

But Pedro did not come home and the official announcement of his death in *The Times* brought forth another avalanche of letters, including one from the King and Queen. On 17 July 1945 Patricia was invited to Buckingham Palace to receive from King George VI, Pedro's insignia of the Distinguished Service Order and the decoration of the Distinguished Flying Cross with its Bar.

The last words on this short but remarkable life are contributed most fittingly by two of Pedro's most highly decorated comrades in 260 Squadron. In July 2008 Wing Commander (Retired) J.F. (Eddie) Edwards DFC and Bar, DFM wrote from Canada:

'I considered him a very great leader, absolutely fearless. He was a very private person, not long on briefings. But he showed by good example; a gentleman, excellent pilot and a good shot. We respected and liked him and most of all we would follow him anywhere.'

Similarly, from Australia, Flight Lieutenant (Retired) W.R. (Ron) Cundy DFC DFM wrote to say:

'I believe he was the only man I ever met who was genuinely without fear. No matter what the circumstances he showed no sign of panic or any trace of nervousness. In addition there was no sign of bravado and certainly not braggadocio. As I said in my book [A Gremlin on My Shoulder] *Pedro was without a doubt the finest commanding officer under whom I ever served. He insisted on strict discipline both in the air and on the ground but was always eminently fair. He seemed to be possessed of dauntless courage and no matter what the situation, never panicked.'*

EPILOGUE

MISSING

' *Missing*', says the telegram. Great God,
it can't be so!
He seems so close; we saw him such a little
time ago.
His features are so vivid and his memory
so clear.
His personality still clings to every object
near.

Was that goodbye for ever?
No, there must be some mistake.
Can a person go on living
When their heart begins to break?

But we shall always see him in familiar
things we touch.
His deeds will live while we live because we
loved so much.
And we shall go on smiling – he would hate
to see our tears,
And keep our thoughts of him until we
share eternal years.'

Claim List of Osgood Villiers Hanbury
RAF Numbers: 742867 (NCO); 81357 (Officer)

Claim		Type of aircraft	Aircraft identification	Location
1940				
7 Sep	**602 Sqn**			
Do17 Damaged		Spitfire I	N3228	Biggin Hill area
12 Sep	**602 Sqn** ⅓			
Do17 Damaged		Spitfire I	X4162	Beachy Head
15 Sep	**602 Sqn**			
Bf110		Spitfire I	X4382	Beachy Head
21 Sep	**602 Sqn** ½			
Ju88		Spitfire I	X4382	Tangmere
30 Sep	**602 Sqn**			
Ju88		Spitfire I		Selsey-Bembridge
5 Oct	**602 Sqn** ½			
Ju88 Damaged		Spitfire I	X4382	S Beachy Head
30 Oct	**602 Sqn**			
Bf109E		Spitfire I	X4162	Robertsbridge-Dungeness
1941				
14 Dec	**260 Sqn**			
Ju87		Hurricane I	Z4804	Gazala
Bf109 Damaged		Hurricane I		Z4804

APPENDIX

1942

3 Apr   260 Sqn ½
Bf109   Kittyhawk Ia   AK867   5m NW Bomba

25 Apr   260 Sqn
Ju87   Kittyhawk Ia   AK801   Tobruk-Gazala
MC202   Kittyhawk Ia   Tobruk-Gazala
MC202 Probable   Kittyhawk Ia   Tobruk-Gazala

27 Jun   260 Sqn
Bf109   Kittyhawk Ia   Fuka
Bf109 Probable   Kittyhawk Ia   Fuka

6 Jul   260 Sqn
Bf109   Kittyhawk Ia   ET575   E El Daba

14 Dec   260 Sqn
Bf109 Damaged   Kittyhawk II

1943

2 Jan   260 Sqn
Bf109   Kittyhawk III   Churgia

17 Apr   260 Sqn
Bf110   Kittyhawk III   N Cap Bon

TOTAL: 10 and 2 shared destroyed, 2 probables, 3 and 2 shared damaged.

INDEX

166